The Prehistoric Sites of the Gower & West Glamorgan

Monuments in the Landscape

Volume VII

The Prehistoric Sites of the Gower & West Glamorgan

by
Wendy Hughes

Logaston Press

LOGASTON PRESS
Little Logaston Woonton Almeley
Herefordshire HR3 6QH

First published by Logaston Press 1999
Copyright © Wendy Hughes 1999

ISBN 1 873827 75 X

Set in Times 11pt by Logaston Press
and printed in Great Britain by
The Cromwell Press, Wiltshire

Contents

Please Note

Where monuments mentioned in this book are situated on private land, permission from the owner must be obtained before visiting them. The following points must be observed:

1. Always follow the Countryside Code.

2. On all sites, extreme care should be taken.

3. Any artefacts found on sites in the Gower or West Glamorgan should be reported to the Glamorgan and Gwent Archaeological Trust, Ferryside Warehouse, Bath Lane, Swansea SA1 1RD, or at any local museum.

4. Under no circumstances should visitors dig on or around any site. Any damage could result in prosecution.

5. It is an offence under the 1979 Ancient Monuments and Archaeological Areas Act to use metal detectors on or near scheduled ancient monuments. In addition, simple 'treasure hunting' near ancient monuments can well damage evidence to such an extent that archaeologists are unable to interpret it fully in the future.

Acknowledgements

I would like to thank, firstly, all the archaeologists who have worked so hard, and often not in pleasant conditions, to piece together the past and bring it alive for the general public.

Secondly, I would like to thank all historians and writers, past and present, who have contributed so much to our knowledge and without who's 'indirect' help I would not have been able to even contemplate such a book. Any errors and omissions are of my own doing, and if I have inadvertently allowed any to creep into my text, I do apologise.

I would also like to thank the contributors of *Archaeologia Cambrensis*, who have furthered my knowledge, The Glamorgan and Gwent Archaeological Trust Ltd for their help in dealing with queries so promptly, and also the British Library in London.

A special thanks to Conrad Hughes who has had to live and breathe the prehistoric times for many years now and take various sojourns into West Glamorganshire to enable me to check out a piece of information or view a site.

Thanks are also due to The Royal Commission on the Ancient and Historical Monuments of Wales at Plas Crug, Aberystwyth for the various photographs which are credited to them in the text. Also to Brian Byron for drawing the overall location map.

Finally, an extra special thank you to Andy Johnson and Ron Shoesmith for their time and valuable editorial comments, which have enhanced the text and I hope your enjoyment of this book.

Wendy Hughes
March 1999

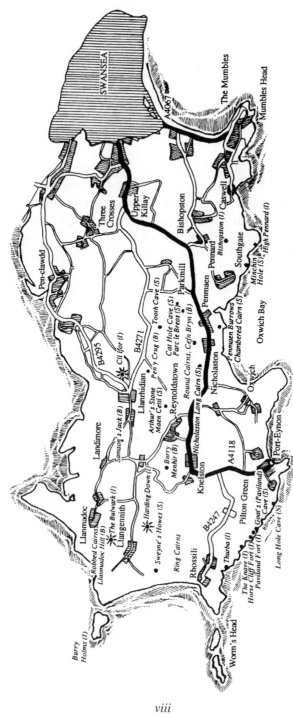

Map of The Gower showing Stone Age (S), Bronze Age (B)
and Iron Age (I) sites described in the gazetteer

Introduction

This book covers the Gower Peninsula and Glamorganshire west of the river Neath; that is the entire territory of the Old Lordship of Gower including the region between the rivers Tawe and Neath, extending from Pontardawe in the north to the westernmost tip of the Gower Peninsula. It is an area rich in prehistoric sites and from the artefacts recovered archaeologists have been able to learn much about the environment of those times, as well as how people lived and died.

The Gower Peninsula itself covers a relatively small area of land comprising of an outstretched arm of some 20km of limestone, yet it has an abundance of prehistoric sites and monuments that reflect on a long and complex history of man's existence. North of the Gower lies a fertile coastal plain with wide estuaries, a land suitable for settlement by early man who largely used waterways as his lines of travel. These early Palaeolithic (Old Stone Age) adventurous cave dwellers were perceptive enough to know that it would make an ideal hunting ground and a permanent home. In turn the Neolithic (New Stone Age) settlers with their farming skills and unique style of burial chamber, the Bronze Age people with their cairns and circles, as well as the builders of the Iron Age hillforts continued to make it their home.

Over the years prehistoric man, justly or unjustly, has had to put up with a bad press, often being portrayed by illustrators as an 'uncouth' savage wielding a stone axe, dragging his partner around by her hair and communicating by a series of grunts. However, finds from a burial site in a cave at Paviland on the Gower Peninsula demonstrate that this cave man had friends who cared enough about him to give him a special burial, although we still have much to learn about their rituals.

The prehistoric monuments in the ancient county of West Glamorganshire can be divided roughly into two broad sections—

settlements and burial or commemorative sites. Many of the settlements were used for several generations and tell us a great deal about their occupants, whilst others, especially the caves and promontory forts, were used as temporary shelters in times of troubles.

Now, thanks to the painstaking work of archaeologists, there is a basic understanding of the landscape in which early man lived and died, and I hope by the end of this book that if you had the perception of early man as a bunch of uncouth savages who practised cannibalism, you'll instead learn to marvel at their ingenuity, their survival abilities and interpret the magical landscape for yourself.

Wendy Hughes
March 1999

The Stone Ages

The Ice Age to the Palaeolithic

To appreciate and enjoy some of the artefacts found in and around the monuments in Glamorganshire, it is necessary to take a step back in time to see what the environment would have looked like to our prehistoric ancestors.

500,000 years ago longer periods of much colder and drier conditions alternated with periods when the British climate was much hotter than anything experienced today; indeed it was almost equatorial weather. This would account for the seemingly disparate collection of animal bones discovered in the area, especially on the Gower Peninsula. In the 'Ice Age' the woolly mammoth, cave bear and giant reindeer would have adapted to the sub zero temperatures, whilst the rhinoceros, straight tusked elephant, lion and hippopotamus would have enjoyed basking in the warmer climate. Vast collections of animal bones belonging to these species are on display in Swansea Museum, the National Museum of Wales at Cardiff, as well as the British Museum in London.

The term Ice Age can be a little misleading, for in southern Britain and north-west Europe the climate during this time was essentially cold and dry, producing a treeless tundra with an abundance of grasses and herbs. However, these conditions alternated with widespread glaciation, as well as warmer periods that resulted in the rapid spread of forests and vegetation.

Britain was once a peninsula of mainland Europe, and at the end of the last Ice Age, huge cliffs swept down from the edge of the wind-swept Gower Peninsula towards a wide valley. Much of the Gower Peninsula consisted of carboniferous limestone, a hard grey rock, which, despite its hardness, dissolves in water. Water seeped

1

between the fissures and bedding planes of the stone, and over many thousands of years sufficient rock dissolved to leave large cavities. These in turn made ideal cave shelters for the early inhabitants. Today, these caves do not allow easy access, their entrances being on the cliff faces that look out over the waters of the Bristol Channel which now divide Wales from the West Country. It was in this valley (now the Bristol Channel) that some of the exotic animals—whose remains survive to the present day—would have roamed. It is highly unlikely that some of the larger animals actually lived or died in the caves; the presence of their bones can be explained as either the work of carnivorous animals such as the wolf, who would have dragged the carcass into the cave, or of the groups of hunters who occupied the caves.

Early Man—*Homo Erectus* to Neanderthal

Nomadic groups of hunters moved widely over Northern Europe and braved the elements in pursuit of seasonal migration of herds, such as those of mammoth, reindeer, wild horse, bison and even elephant. This primitive species of man, known as *Homo Erectus*, was the not-quite-so-human offspring of the ape. In many ways they resembled a strongly built version of their direct descendent, modern man.

By about 300,000 BC *Homo Erectus* was slowly evolving, but evolution developed at varying rates in different places, and some would have taken a different route from the path by which most evolved. There were many reasons which influenced these changes, one being the mutation of genes. There is a possibility that some groups became totally isolated and their development became static, eventually becoming extinct. Some of the more intelligent groups learned to craft tools for work that had once been performed by teeth or muscles, and over the centuries this affected their physical development.

How quickly or slowly these people evolved is open to speculation. Life would not have been easy for early man, and the only tools and weapons they used were made of stone or flint. The earliest hand-axes they shaped consisted merely of a fist-size lump of stone or flint chipped into a head resembling a flattened pear. Despite its simplicity, it was an extremely useful tool and experiments suggest that it also served as a butcher's knife to cut up carcasses which had already been skinned by using sharp, flat stone flakes. These old stone tools, which also consisted of cleavers and scrapers, were called Acheulean tools after the 300,000 year-old finds from St. Acheul in northern France.

There is no evidence to prove conclusively that this early man actually settled in Glamorganshire, but there is evidence of his presence in the county thanks to two isolated finds, one at Pen-y-lan, Cardiff, and the other near Rhossili on the Gower Peninsula. At Pen-y-lan an Acheulean quartzite hand-axe belonging to the Lower Palaeolithic period is estimated to date from 200,000 BC.[1] The chipped stone tool discovered at Rhossili in 1978 is the earliest piece of evidence to indicate man's presence on the Gower Peninsula. This primitive stone implement is a hand held axe and archaeologists believe it was made some time in the Lower Palaeolithic period. However, one cave dwelling at Pontnewydd near St. Asaph in North Wales did reveal more substantial evidence, which included hand-axes dating to around 230,000 BC. They were discovered by Sir William Boyd Dawkins along with the bones of *Rhinoceros merckii*, a species which distinctively belongs to the warm or pre-glacial period.

What does this lack of evidence mean? It could indicate that, due to the absence in South Wales of natural flint for early Palaeolithic implements, man was discouraged from settling, or possibly that they did settle but used a more perishable tool which has been lost. It could also have been due to the fact that animal life in Wales was scant and therefore not worth pursuing. However, it is still possible that they did settle and that some, as yet, undiscovered evidence of their existence lurks in the deep recesses of a Welsh cave.

From evidence uncovered at sites across Europe it has been established that these people were mainly scavengers and plant gatherers, though it is evident, from the collection of bones and stone tools found, that they also hunted in groups. It is likely that the men would have been at 'home' for just a few days, long enough to plan and execute a hunt. It is also likely that the hunters would have brought their spoils home, butchered the animals and shared out the meat. They would have quenched their thirst at the nearby stream or lake, and told heroic tales around a flickering campfire. After resting they would have refurbished their tools and started out again.

It is not certain if early man discovered how to make a fire or were dependent on those already started by lightning or the odd volcanic eruption, but we do know that he used fire—for warmth, cooking and as a protective weapon to scare and drive away wild animals.

Many palaeo-anthropologists believe that the majority of people from the last Ice Age were of the same species—an archaic form of *Homo Sapiens*, a direct ancestor of modern man. However, as mentioned, there were other side branches along the evolution path, and one of these, some claim, was Neanderthal Man who lived around 100,000 BC.

The name Neanderthal is derived from the Neander valley near Düsseldorf, in western Germany, where portions of a male skeleton were taken from a limestone cave besides the river in 1857. This skeleton, together with a woman's skull found in 1848 in a quarry in Gibraltar, and another found lying un-described and unstudied, in Stuttgart Museum, played a major role in helping to define the species.

A minority of anthropologists believe that Neanderthal Man became extinct by about 30,000 BC and was replaced by modern man. Others suggest that they interbred, or evolved into a sub-species. It is known that their genes survive in people alive today, so it appears that only further research and the continual re-assessment of the evidence will reveal a fuller picture.

Neanderthal man sometimes lived in caves, but more often in temporary shelters erected near and around rivers and lakes. These shelters were made from animal hides hung from a central pole and weighted down. Remains of a number of these weights have been found in Spain, but none, as yet, in Wales. Perhaps those who visited Glamorganshire were content to live in the abundance of ready-made shelters in the limestone outcrops? Or perhaps any evidence of their dwellings has been swept away by a later Ice Age?

When the deep snows of winter arrived and the edible plants became scarce, man would have been forced to rely more on meat, and may have resorted to cannibalism. Neanderthal man was more adventurous and hunted far less haphazardly than his predecessor. He also knew a great deal about animal behaviour and used it to the best of his ability. From the evidence left behind at his kill sites, and remains scattered around his hearths we can deduce a great deal.

Amongst the blackened remains of campfires found throughout Europe, there has been discovered the bones of reindeer, horse, ibex, elephant, elk, bear, and the now extinct woolly rhinoceros, mammoth, as well as the cattle-like aurochs. Hunts would have been planned accordingly and the methods used became more ingenious, including hurling spears, rolling boulders off cliffs, or setting snares and pitfall traps. For example, a sharpened piece of yew, believed to be 300,000 years old, found at Clacton-on-Sea and preserved because the site was waterlogged, may have come from a spear. The tip had been dried by holding it over a flame, rendering it hard enough to penetrate the hides of animals. The hunters would have learned how to pick off the easy prey, like the sick, weak, old and young animals. They learnt that fire could drive whole herds to the edge of cliffs or into dead-end canyons for mass slaughter. Although Neanderthal man's preference was for big game hunting, because it provided nourishment for more people, smaller animals and birds were also hunted, and no doubt the youngsters in the group would have learnt the basic skills of survival from hunting small, easy prey.

Methods of tool-making had developed through various stages and techniques too. One of the oldest methods, as mentioned, was the Acheulean method. However, much later the method favoured by most was the Mousterian method, so named after tools found in 1860 in the caves at Le Moustier, France. Unlike the earlier tools, which were made by shaping stone, these were made of stone flakes. These flakes were obtained by knocking off flake after flake from the core stone, the flakes then being taken back to the home base to be further worked to obtain the sharpened edges needed for working with wood, hide or carcasses. This basic flaking technique, called *levallois*, enabled man to make the refinements required to produce thin-bladed points and double-edged scrapers.

Just outside the area covered by this book, but within sight of Burry Holms at the far extremity of the Gower Peninsula, sits Coygan Cave in a steep-faced outcrop of carboniferous limestone. This site was first excavated between 1963-65 and Mousterian flaked flint tools and hand-axes were discovered as well as evidence of occupation.[2] Also a single chert flake, belonging to this Mousterian *levallois* technique was found at Goat's Cave, Paviland, demonstrating that early man had at least roamed this part of the county.

But however advanced these people may seem, early man managed to grasp neither the potential of bone as a material for tools, nor the art of sewing. Garments were fashioned by using animal skins and stone tools. First the hide would have been laid flat and, with the aid of a stone scraper, the fat and flesh removed. After the skin had been cleaned it would have been cured in the smoke of a smouldering fire to toughen it and seal the pores. It is likely that the pieces for the garment were cut up with a flaked stone knife and holes punched along the edges of the skins with a pointed stone. The pieces were then laced together with narrow strips of rawhide—to form a sort of skin toga. Shoes were made the same way. It is highly likely that when they skinned the smaller animals such as foxes, hares and wolves, they would have left the feet intact to serve as ties.

We know very little about early man's living customs—any evidence of late Neanderthal or early Palaeolithic flimsy encampments would have been swept away by the re-appearance of the glaciers during the last Ice Age. But we do know a little about their burial rituals. Around 150 bodies have already been found in Europe and almost all have been found deliberately buried in caves,

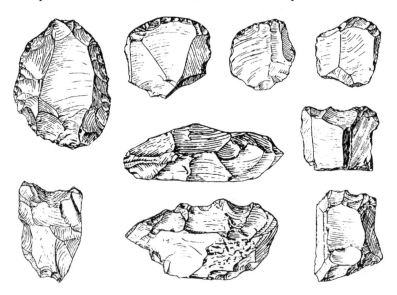

Examples of flint scrapers found in Paviland Cave

indeed in Britain all have been found buried in caves. It could be that caves were favoured as burial sites partly for convenience, as they were a ready-made shelter. It could also be that because the group returned to these caves during seasonal hunts that, as well as providing a base for the living, it also allowed them to maintain a link with their ancestors—and the caves were a readily recognisable feature in the landscape whilst a burial site in the surrounding wilderness may soon have become lost to the group's consciousness. Caves also have an 'air of mystery' about them and that may have made them suitable dwellings for the dead.

The dead were buried in graves dug into the floor of the cave, their bodies placed in the sleeping position and provided with stone tools, roasted meat and a stone pillow. Some lay on a bed of woody horsetail, whilst others were covered with a thin scattering of late spring flowers, detectable by their pollen grains.

Early to Late Upper Palaeolithic Period—The Cave Dwellers
Fortunately caves used as burial sites as well as for shelter at the onset of the last glaciation are in an abundance in the area covered by this book. Thanks to radio-carbon methods, the earliest can be dated to the Early Upper Palaeolithic period—36,000 to 25,000 BC.

Around 20,000 BC Britain suffered another glaciation, and sheets of ice covered the country to within a few miles of the southern edge of the Gower Peninsula. The animal remains that have been found suggest that the landscape was similar to that of present day Greenland, the local environment treeless and open with low bushy vegetation, such as willow, juniper and dwarf birch. Most of these finds have come from some of the 95 known limestone caves scattered around the Gower. It is estimated that around 22 of these show traces of occupation, some of which date from this very early period.

At this time the population of the whole of Britain is estimated to have numbered around 500 and that only about 50 people would have been in this area at any given time.[3] These figures, used in context, provide us with an appreciation of just how remarkable these finds are.

Before this last Ice Age, as indicated by finds of flint flakes, some people did frequent Goat's Hole at Paviland (SS 437 859). However, more important, are the human remains found here in

1823 which date to around 26,550 BC. This first known 'Welshman' was discovered by Professor Buckland. The skeleton was later examined by Professor W.J. Sollas and found to belong to the Upper Palaeolithic.[4]

As yet, no other remains have been found in Britain between then and 17,000 BC and it is apparent that for this ten thousand year period most of Britain and northern Europe was in the grip of a severe Ice Age. At its height, ice sheets around 400m thick would have covered all of Wales, most of the west of England and would have engulfed the Wash and the North Sea.

By 16,000 BC the ice rapidly began to melt and southern Britain was soon colonised by sub-arctic tundra plants which, in time, encouraged animals such as elk, reindeer and horse to return. This in turn would have brought small hunting communities to the area. It is also possible that small, food gathering groups lived contentedly near the shore of the rising post-glacial sea without much communication with the more mobile hunters of game.

Evidence from beetle remains and pollen grains show that by 12,000 BC warmer conditions had returned to Britain. This phase is known as the Late Upper Palaeolithic period, and is the period when man returned to Gower and other parts of Glamorganshire. During this period it seems that Cat Hole Cave (SS 538 901) in Parkmill was occupied, and although today little visual evidence of that occupation remains, it is still an interesting experience to enter Cat Hole and to try to imagine the conditions under which our early ancestors lived. In contrast Long Hole Cave (SS 452 851) in Port Eynon shows no signs of settled occupation, although evidence points to it being used as a small hunting camp.

Although the warmer climate was essentially here to stay, there was one short and severe cold phase, known as the Loch Lomond stadial, which occurred between 11,000 and 10,000 BC. After this 'blip' the climate gradually continued to improve, and this brought a completely new set of flora to the landscape, such as lime and elder.

The Mesolithic or Middle Stone Age—The Hunter Gatherers
This warmer climate brought a further increase in vegetation, and thick woodlands, formed of hazel, elm and oak, would have encouraged a variety of animals to settle. Although the weather was still

8

cooler, though drier than today, by the end of the Mesolithic (4,000 BC) an Atlantic climate would have existed and supported a thick deciduous forest.

The great mammals of the Early Upper Palaeolithic became extinct during the Ice Age and were replaced by the animals that are known today, including some no longer found in the wild in Britain, such as bears and lions. The Mesolithic hunter's main enemies would have been the wolves that hunted in packs and the occasional brown bear.

The whereabouts of these Mesolithic 'hunter-gatherers' on the landscape can be traced by the discovery of their flint tools and the waste from their manufacture. It is from this discarded equipment that their hunting techniques can be fully appreciated. The ploughing of the uplands of Gower, which began in the 1960s, has revealed thousands upon thousands of flints at Burry Holms, Cat Hole and Mewslade. These microliths, or micro-blades, 2-4cm long, made of flint and shaped by further chipping into various forms, have been left scattered around occupation areas in vast quantities. The majority were pointed although some were blunted across one end. Others were more elaborately worked and shaped into triangles and crescents. The microliths are characteristic of the Mesolithic and became even finer towards the end of the period. They were set as barbs along the shaft of a wooden spear, and would frequently break off when the thrown spear missed its target and struck something hard like a stone—giving rise to the abundance of broken microliths now found.

Another traditional piece of hunting equipment from this period is the pointed, barbed weapon made of bone or antler. These are often referred to as harpoons, but there is no provision for attaching a line, so we do not know for certain if they were used for fishing or only for spearing animals. Although fish are known to have provided an important supplement to the human diet, fish bones and scales are very fragile and are rarely preserved.

Hunting animals and gathering fruits and plants remained a way of life for these tribal communities, and by studying the remains of butchered animals from this period scientists have been able to find out a great deal about the lifestyle of these early people. For example, many of the foot bones of horses and red deer found have cut marks on the underside of their toes. It has been suggested that the long tendons were extracted by careful cutting of the feet and then used as a thread for sewing hides to make clothing or for binding a spearhead to a shaft.

Finely polished bone sewing needles have been found on the Gower, indicating that these hunters were better clothed than their predecessors, but how they made the eye of the needle is uncertain. Some believe that a crude pointed boring tool was used, in much the same way as a gimlet is used today. Others argue that perhaps a primitive type of rotary drill had been invented. However they were made, these bone needles, together with the sinews of animals, were used to join pieces of skin to make a variety of garments.

The campsite would have been a busy place with old equipment being repaired and new items made, whilst food was prepared and stored. Meat and fish was dried and smoked in order to provide the group with security against leaner times. Much of their day would have been taken up with the routine preparation and cooking of foods and this would have required a constant supply of firewood and water. All the known Mesolithic sites are close to a fresh water supply, but even so, some sort of container would have been needed to carry the water any distance. It is likely that leather bags or animal bladders were used for this purpose, but no such items have survived.

For relaxation it is almost certain that they would have entertained themselves with story telling, music and dancing, and there may have even been events to encourage friendship, marriage and the exchange of the odd gift or two between members of each group. But life would not have always been so sanguine. There may also have been bitter battles between rival groups, as well as hunting competitions, and famine due to weather conditions would have taken their toll on the people too.

By now tool making had become more sophisticated as indicated by the beautifully crafted art objects found, which have included animal and human figures. Artefacts of this period are recorded as belonging to the Creswellian period, after the first such items found in the Creswell Crags on the borders of Derbyshire and Nottinghamshire.

The Mesolithic peoples were also the first to produce cave art although none has been discovered in the Glamorganshire area.

However, in 1912 there was much excitement in Gower when ten strange, horizontal bands of dark red markings were discovered in a cavern in Bacon Hole (SS 560 868) in the cliff face west of Hunts Bay, just half a mile from Pennard. Could these series of lines have represented a net or a trap for catching big game? Could more paintings like those found at Lascaux in France lurk in the deep recesses of these Glamorganshire caves? The Welsh experts were unsure, so they invited the French expert, Abbé Breuil to examine the scratchings. After careful consideration he rubbed his chin, and said there was a possibility that they could be. The archaeologists were delighted and immediately placed an iron grille around the markings to protect them. But, as the years passed, the lines slowly changed shape. Finally, it was discovered that they were caused by iron oxide seeping naturally from the rocks. Sadly Glamorganshire didn't enter the history books alongside Lascaux. Today the iron grille is broken and rusted, a fading relic to what might have been.

The cave, named after the red oxide streaks, was first excavated in the 1850s by Col. E.R. Wood. He found animal remains, including an antler which bore the marks of carving[5] and a bowl from the Palaeolithic period, as well as an Irish seventh century brooch—clear indication that man had once inhabited the cave, and had continued to do so for many generations. A more extensive investigation also produced a fine collection of animal bones, including those of a giant ox, bison, wolf, soft-nosed rhinoceros, and a hyena. They are now exhibited in Swansea Museum.

By 5,000 BC Glamorganshire was enjoying a more hospitable climate. The weather continued to improve and an even more varied plant life began to flourish. By now animals such as reindeer and mammoth, which were more comfortable with a colder climate, had headed north and man was left to develop the landscape and its natural resources as best he could. However, little is known of this later Mesolithic period because very few well-preserved sites with artefacts have been discovered or indeed excavated. Again only time will reveal more.

The New Stone Age or Neolithic—From Hunters to Farmers
Sometime between 4,400 and 3,000 BC man began to domesticate animals and agriculture on a small scale was adopted, the popula-

11

tion moving slowly from the Mesolithic to the Neolithic, or the New Stone Age period. This transition would have been gradual and was also heralded by the arrival of small bands of people from Spain, Portugal, and the countries bordering the Mediterranean Sea, who were migrating across Europe. These people, who were short, dark haired and long headed, migrated northwards using the sea as a useful highway. The reason for the migration is unclear. Mr. H.J.E. Peake has suggested the theory that they came in search of amber, fossilised tree resin. However, other factors need to be considered such as famine in other parts of Europe, or even man's instinct for adventure.

By now the climate was warmer and wetter, making Britain a perfect region to grow crops such as wheat and barley. It was also close to the sea and rivers, which made it an ideal location for the pearl-fisher. Perhaps this lured people north. However, the evidence is scanty, for there are only a few shell-mounds and so-called Neolithic hearths in south Wales. All of the latter are located around the coast, suggesting that Neolithic man was a coastal dweller who lived on the cliffs above the sea or along the estuaries, leaving the interior of the country almost uninhabited. The cliffs would have provided him with the source of rock for his implements, the cliff tops and estuaries the pasture on which to graze his animals, and the sea a variety to his diet and possibly protection from unwelcome visitors.

The shell-mounds that have been discovered at Swanlake in Pembrokeshire and at the hearth-places at Burry Holms have revealed flint flakes and early pottery, which could provide us with the clues to, possibly, the first Neolithic settlements in south Wales. The Burry Holms site (SS 399 925) is situated on level ground above a low cliff on the south side of the island. The cliff is being slowly eroded and many of the flint artefacts and waste fragments have been picked up from time to time on the cliff edge. The chipping floor, situated near the top of a low cliff is very exposed, and an unpublished report on an excavation carried out by T.C. Lethbridge and H.E. David in 1923 showed that the flints lay on a glacial drift which tops the limestone bedrock. Some flints showed signs of fire, and although there are no other signs of occupation, it can be assumed that this was a settlement and that any evidence of domestic dwelling can only be recovered by further excavation.

Some flint scrapers, microlithic points and flakes were also collected from this site between 1946-48 by J.G. Rutter and are now in private possession.

The use of plants and tamed animals to provide a more predictable food supply were also being introduced and the archae-ological evidence suggests a gradual process of economic and social change. It has sometimes been suggested that the change from a Mesolithic to a Neolithic way of life was due to a sudden influx of invading warriors, but the change may well have been brought about by an invasion of ideas and not necessarily people. However, it is known that some settlers did arrive, in dug out canoes, with domes-ticated animals, stores of seed grain and general equipment. They were pioneers in a new land with a small native population that presented no threat to them, so it can safely be assumed that the orig-inal inhabitants were either absorbed into the new society or as 'minority citizens' eventually died out. Interestingly, it has been demonstrated that there is a significant difference between the types of monument and pottery styles in the British Neolithic period to those of Europe. Therefore it is far more likely that these new Neolithic settlers were impressed by the existing Mesolithic ideas and culture, and adapted them to suit their own needs.

Flint continued to play an important role in the Neolithic civili-sation of Britain, and evidence of this can be seen in the develop-ment of flint mines in Norfolk, Sussex and Wessex. Flint was exten-sively used for ordinary weapons such as arrowheads, knives and scrapers. The typical arrowhead of the time is the oval or leaf-shaped type of which many have been found in and around the caves of Gower. Flint scrapers were numerous, and as animal skins were still used as clothing they were a vital tool for Neolithic man.

Settlements of Neolithic man in the Glamorganshire area are few, but many of the chipping or working areas found in the sand-dunes of south Wales appear to have been used at this period. One site, at Merthyr Mawr Warren near Porthcawl has produced over 50 arrowheads.[6] On the Gower Peninsula, two sites, one at Pennard Burrows and another at Great Tor, Penmaen have revealed leaf shaped arrowheads in the sand dune region. The Pennard Burrows finds were discovered by Mr. T.H. Tiddeman near the remains of three cairns (SS 539 878) on the top of the cliff on the eastern end

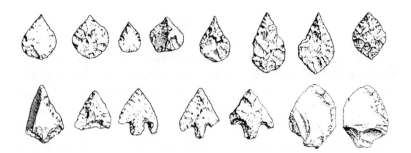

Flint arrowheads from Merthyr Mawr Warren

of Three Cliffs Bay. The finds from the Great Tor site (SS 530 877) included a leaf-shaped arrowhead with the point missing, a flint end scraper and flakes and fragments of un-worked flint, found by Mr. J.G. Rutter in 1946-8 and now in private possession. In 1948 the base of a leaf-shaped arrowhead together with un-worked fragments were found in 1948 by Mr. T.R. Webber and are now also in private possession.[7]

Late Farmers — The Age of Advancement

These small communities had a considerable impact on the countryside. They were not only our first farmers, but were also our first builders. The oak and hazel trees that had given the early settlers protection from the climate and inter-tribal warfare were no longer needed. Forest clearance began in earnest. Man soon learned that by attaching a wooden handle to his stone axe he could clear the dense forests, such as those that existed in the Vale of Glamorganshire, much quicker. However, to date, the only Neolithic axe found in a Gower cave is a single head-axe made of Graig Lwyd stone. This polished specimen, presumably from a neighbouring settlement, could have been originally traded from the Graig Lwyd axe factory in North Wales,[8] or it could have been a gift from another tribal chief. It is now clear that this north Wales Neolithic factory catered for 'national' as well as local needs. Axes from Graig Lwyd have been discovered as far afield as Avebury, Wiltshire, and Windmill Hill, Devon, which also suggests that there was much movement of people during this time, or increased trading activity.

With the eventual introduction of agriculture, cattle, pigs and, to a lesser degree, sheep and goats, were brought from Spain and Portugal. The uplands were used mainly for hunting and as a rich source of fine stone used in the manufacture of tools and weapons. Men became expert farmers and learned to domesticate animals rather than hunt them. Women learned to make rope from horsehair and began to master the craft of weaving woollen cloth. It is not known when textiles were first introduced, but spun thread was certainly being manufactured in the later Neolithic period because spindle whorls, the small flywheel that fits over the end of the spindle used during the making of the thread, have been found at a number of Welsh sites. As flax was cultivated it can also be assumed that perhaps under-garments were worn, not necessarily by all, but at least by some of the more important members of the community.

As a community these people now had an alternative to the leather garments worn by their predecessors. They also made pottery, and placed wooden handles on their flint weapons but, as yet, knew nothing about metals.

The major change in food-supply bound man to one place for at least as long as the crops took to ripen, as opposed to the length of a hunt, or the time it took to preserve the next food supply. This changed the way of life to a predominantly settled farming one. Now settlements, usually comprising of one or two wooden houses enclosed with a ditch and causewayed entrance, began to establish a more civil and community life. Civilisation as we know it today had begun.

Little is known of settlements in the area, but occasionally a settlement is found by chance like the one found in 1958 at Sant-y-nyll (ST 100 782) north-east of St. Brides-Super-Ely near Cardiff. An oval ring of post holes representing a hut, and some domestic refuse containing 500

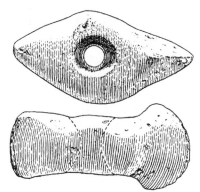

*Stone axe-hammer from
Llanmadoc, Gower*

bones of sheep, ox and wild boar indicated a small farming community. Interestingly three claws of a brown bear were also found, along with a small number of scrapers and flakes.[9] Another settlement, outside the county at Clegr Boia, near St. David's in Pembrokeshire, was excavated in 1943. This consisted of two Neolithic house structures, a fire pit and a domestic midden.[10]

In Britain, in contrast with much of Europe, the evidence for farming during this period has been scant. There is little evidence of settlements and of any associated fields. As a result, a small scale study was carried out on the bones of 23 Neolithic people from ten sites in central and southern England. By looking at one particular isotope in the bone's protein it can tell us, by comparison with values obtained from known herbivores and known carnivores, the rough balance of man's then diet. A group of human bones from the Iron Age were also tested, giving results that suggested a high herbivore diet, confirming the archaeological evidence that cereal production was well under way by then. However, the results from the Neolithic group indicated a diet that relied heavily on meat and/or animal by-products, such as milk and cheese, for the isotope analysis can not distinguish between a diet of meat or of animal by products.[11]

Animal remains from the Neolithic in Britain are generally of domesticated species, even if of a fairly rugged variety—their bones indicate much larger animals than those domesticated during the Iron Age, for example. Agricultural implements, such as the plough, have also been found at Neolithic sites and certainly the isotope analysis suggests some grain was eaten. However, archaeologists such as Richard Bradley and Julian Thomas have argued that in Britain, and elsewhere towards the edge of Europe, that grain was grown, or even imported, largely for ritual purposes, and that agricultural implements may also have assumed a largely ritual significance, citing certain excavation evidence.

With the lack of economic and settlement evidence to confidently guide us through this period, it is necessary to turn attention to the monuments commemorating the dead, which have survived in significant numbers in West Glamorganshire. Originally these monuments, usually consisting of an artificial cave or cell formed of large stones, would have been covered by a mound of earth, leaving the entrance or forecourt area as the only part visible. Archaeological evidence suggests that these tombs may have been used for social, symbolic and political functions as well as a resting place for the dead. Although there is still much to learn about their lifestyle, it has been established that these later Neolithic farmers were religious people who believed in an afterlife. The burial chambers are thought to have been used for many hundreds of years to symbolise the continuity and permanence of a particular clan, and are known to have been the burial places of the men whose culture preceded the introduction of beakers and bronze workings.

Chambered Tombs
Much can be deduced from the 14 surviving tombs in the Glamorganshire area, particularly the two most outstanding, Parc le Breos within the area of this book, and Tinkinswood which is just outside. Most of these tombs are found along the coast with the greatest concentration on the Gower Peninsula, and are extremely rare in other counties of Wales. It is clear from the structures and their contents that these monuments played a very important part in the life of the Neolithic people. They were imposing and carefully built and became the fixed points for a scattered, partly mobile population. They contained the bones of their ancestors, and as such were the key to descent and their relationship with the land. All these tombs are sited on the lower-lying carboniferous limestone or keupar marl regions with their pleasanter climate, and avoid the more exposed rock above the coal measures which form the upland region of north Glamorgan. These tombs are not uniform in design, though they all share the common purpose of being accessible for further burials. Most were covered with a mound of stones (a cairn) or earth (a barrow), which was occasionally circular, but more commonly oblong in shape.

Broadly speaking the tombs in the Glamorganshire area fall into the Severn-Cotswold Group in that all 14 are communal graves with a burial chamber or chambers mostly constructed in the Severn-Cotswold style of massive stones with stone slab capping, completed with drystone walling. The human skulls and bones point to a general population of dark, long-headed people of small stature—typical of the Neolithic period.

The most outstanding and best-preserved of these long cairns is the one at Parc le Breos which has a transepted (short-armed) terminal chamber. It is a wedged-shaped cairn with a smooth fronted, curved forecourt at the broad end, and a passage with four transept chambers, which is a classic design associated with the Severn-Cotswold group. Not far away, the two transepted chambered and passage tomb uncovered on Penmaen Burrows in 1893 (SS 531 881) is clearly part of the same classic form. Two other tombs, Tinkinswood and St. Lythans (ST 100 722) near Cardiff are also in the same Group and, although not in the scope of this book, are of interest. Tinkinswood Chamber (ST 092 733), boasts the largest capstone in Britain. It weighs 40 tons, measures 7.4m x 4.5m, and it has been estimated that about 200 men would have been required to lift it into position using ropes, primitive pulleys, levers and planks. It was first excavated in 1914 by J. Ward when it was revealed as a communal tomb of the Severn-Cotswold tradition. Inside and nearby were found 920 pieces of human bone, nearly all broken, which came from at least 50 people. Eight were certainly youngsters, 21 were females, and 16 males; whilst the rest could not be clearly identified. Pottery found with the bones include fragments of bowls of early Neolithic ware, some of which lay on the floor of the forecourt front, while fragments of a beaker style indicate a later Neolithic use of the tomb.[12] Like Parc le Breos, Tinkinswood tomb was probably used by a small community over a long time, possibly to the end of the Neolithic period. The chambered long tomb at St. Lythans may have once resembled Tinkinswood in plan, but there is no trace of revetment. Today it stands alone, dominating the landscape. There appears to be a low, roughly rectangular mound or platform stretching out to the west of the chamber, and an almost square chamber with a probable entrance on its east side. It may never have been fully covered. Human remains and coarse pottery ware were found on this site in 1875.[13] By the early nineteenth century this tomb was called the 'greyhound bitch kennel' and was used as an animal shelter.

Two other cairns belong to the Severn-Cotswold group in terms of a development of the general type. One, an elongated cairn at Nicholaston (SS 507 888), has been excavated and has a rough stone kerb that defines the mounds. The other, at Tythegston (SS

864 792), has not been excavated. The chamber is the only visible structure, marked by a large capstone lying in a hollow. There is no apparent access to the rectangular chamber within. A slab, 60m away, may once have been robbed from the chamber.

A long mound at Upper Killay (SS 584 922) could also have been a megalithic tomb or long cairn. It was situated on level ground overlooking the broad head of Bishopston valley and was formally described as 'the remains of a long barrow'. In 1959 the much disturbed mound of stone was still visible, but by 1965 the site was occupied by two bungalows, and nothing remains today.

Oval and Round Chambered Tombs

Around 3,000 BC a new series of tombs, known as round barrows, made their appearance. These were highly regionalised and a development of the earlier passage grave which they gradually replaced. The three remaining round barrows of any note in Glamorganshire today are all in western Gower. Maen Cetti, or Arthur's Stone (SS 491 905) stands as a fine example of a type of cairn where the ground from under a large slab was excavated and the sides underpinned with upright stones, as opposed to the slab being raised onto uprights erected on open ground.

There is also a group of cairns on the ridge at Cefn Bryn and three of these have been the subject of excavation during the 1980s. The first to be excavated, by Mr. Anthony Ward, was a small cairn to the north-west of Arthur's Stone.[14] It was discovered to be a ring cairn with two entrances, one of which had been deliberately blocked. Its function seems to have been primarily ritual or ceremonial as no trace of internment or burial has been found. Activities within the circle included the lighting of fires against the inner side of the cairn and the deposition of a small amount of burnt bone and charcoal. The monument occupies a natural platform, which has been enhanced by a pocket of soil thrown up by excavations. It is considered that the interior of the monument would have been unsuitable for use for the burial of more than a dozen people. However, its prominent position in the landscape would have allowed the central area between the cairns to have been seen from the surrounding hillside.

In 1982, excavation of the second of these cairns was heralded by torrential rain and thunder—perhaps an indication that the ancestors of Gower were not happy to be disturbed! This cairn lies approximately 200 metres north-west of Arthur's Stone (SS 490 907), and the site is yet another example of a ring cairn. This cairn had a single entrance, to the south, which again had been deliberately blocked, possibly when the site was no longer in use. Evidence of activity is slight, and a small pit close to the inner edge of the north-eastern arc is surrounded by burnt soil and covered by a stone slab. In the final stages of use the interior of the cairn was filled with quartz stone up to the level of the surrounding bank.[15]

The third cairn to be excavated, in the summer of 1983, was the Great Cairn, and is situated directly west of Arthur's Stone. As yet no excavation report has been published.

There are two other round cairns at Rhossili. Sweyne's Howe North and South are both short and oval but, sadly, their outlines are much mutilated and overgrown, and it is now not certain if any access was provided to the chambers of these two cairns.

To understand the significance of these tombs perhaps they should be seen not merely as burial chambers but as churches for the gods of the living as well as the dead. People's lives were then governed mainly by the agricultural year, and the changing seasons would have assumed a special significance to them. Like us they probably would have celebrated the seasons with special customs and feasts, such as midwinter (our Christmas), the sowing season (our Easter), Midsummer (our Ascension) and Harvest (our Michaelmas). They probably also viewed life as a continual cycle of event—birth, life, death, re-birth, life, and so ever on.

Goat's (Paviland) Cave

Cave occupied from the Upper Palaeolithic period
Location: 3km north-west of Port Eynon. (SS 437 859)
Access: Difficult—the cave is halfway up a cliff and can
only be reached at low tide

There is a public footpath signposted to the cave from the B4247 at Pilton Green. However, the cave can only be reached from the beach at low tide, so visitors should be aware of the incoming tides for the unwary can easily be cut off.

Goat's Cave at Paviland is the most famous Upper Palaeolithic site in Britain, and although difficult to visit, is well worth making that special effort. The cave was occupied mainly between 36,000 to 25,000 BC and an impressive 5,042 artefacts have been recovered from the site. In the early nineteenth century bones from extinct animals were discovered by two brothers from the village of Reynoldston. Their finds were brought to the attention of a local geologist, Lewis Weston Dillwyn who, together with Lady Mary Cole and Miss Talbot of Penrice Castle on the Gower Peninsula first excavated the cave in 1822. On hearing of their finds the Reverend William Buckland, the first Professor of Geology at Oxford University, continued the excavations in 1823 and uncovered part of a human skeleton, the skull and right side being missing. It had been buried in the floor of the cave, about half way in, on the left-hand side. The corpse had been laid in the extended position and the bones were stained red. Close to the thigh, presumably originally in a pouch or pocket, were found about two handfuls of small, perfo-

Teeth found in Paviland Cave

rated shells. These may have once formed a waist girdle, although there is no evidence to confirm this theory. Near the ribs were some 40-50 fragments of small cylinder-shaped ivory rods and some small fragments of ivory rings. Alongside lay the bones of mammoth and rhinoceros, a tongue-shaped implement, made of ivory, and possibly an instrument or charm made from the metacarpal bone of the wolf.

Goat's Cave was described by Buckland as a 'hyena's den', and he assumed that the animal bones had been washed in by the tide, or dragged there by animals. The skeleton, which he thought to be that of a young lady, based on the presence of the 'ivory jewellery', was dubbed The Red Lady of Paviland. Because human existence during such an early period was then unthinkable, Buckland assumed the skeleton was that of a priestess from the Romano-British period, and went on to surmise how, one day, a high priestess was walking along the cliffs and fell into the cave where she had lain undiscovered for centuries.

However, in 1912, Professor Sollas of the Geology Department at Oxford re-examined the cave. The cave itself is about 100ft high, 60ft in length and 200ft broad, now some 30-40 feet above the present sea level. In the lifetime of Paviland Man (as he has been nicknamed), the cave would have looked out across a vast wooded, level plain where animals roamed freely, rather than the present aspect of the sea as it is today. From the mouth of the cave the inhabitants could have had an excellent view of their next meal, and would have planned their attack accordingly. Professor Sollas showed that these Paviland cave-dwellers were in the Aurignacian stage of culture (a period of the Palaeolithic named after Aurignac, in the Haute Garonne on the lower slopes of the Pyrenees). He also showed that they had affinities with the tall peoples of Cro-Magnon near Les Eyzies n the valley of the river Vezere, where several skeletons have been found.[16] It would seem that the Aurignacian colonists had walked over the land bridge connecting England and France many centuries before the land sunk and were possibly the first 'Gowerians'.

A large collection of the implements found in the cave were examined by Professors Sollas and Abbé Breuil from France and were classified as belonging to the Early, Middle and Upper

Aurignacian periods, which included characteristic specimens of end scrapers, or flakes, squarish scrapers and circular scrapers. Over 4,000 man-worked flint flakes were found, together with several fragments of worked bone and ivory. Five canine teeth and two of reindeer were perforated and were undoubtedly worn as a necklace. The skeletons found at Cro-Magnon had been buried with 300 pieces of marine shells which had ben strung together to form a necklace. That the Cro-Magnons came into contact with goods if not traders from afar is shown by an excavation at Grimaldi in France where an Indian Ocean shell was found. At Paviland, Professor Sollas found a fragment of ivory that was pierced and had evidently been used as a pendant, but he also noticed that it had been cut from a pulp cavity of a mammoth's tusk which fitted exactly into a piece of deformed tusk discovered in the cave by Buckland over a century earlier.

Professor Sollas also re-examined the bones of the 'lady' and found that 'she' was actually a 'he', a slender young man aged about 25, at least middle-aged by Palaeolithic standards, and a representative of the Cro-Magnon race. For a long time archaeologists believed that the man had died around 16,500 BC, but more recently that date had been revised to around 24,000 BC.

The Cro-Magnons were no mere savages who lived the life of animals, but appeared to have been an exceptional race of people with active and inquiring minds, a high sense of social organisation, and a set of definite beliefs. Presumably the staining of the bones of the Red Lady with red micaceous oxide of iron reflected these beliefs. But what were these beliefs, and did the Cro-Magnon race paint their bodies during life?

Some have suggested that the bones were painted after the flesh had decayed, but there was no indication that the grave had been disturbed after the corpse had been laid to rest. As the earth as well as the bones had retained the colouration, it is more likely that the corpse had been smeared over with red earth which, after the flesh had decayed, fell on the skeleton and the earth beside it. This would mean the red colour was applied before the body was placed in the grave and no doubt was intended to serve a definite purpose. By studying other pagan cultures and the Babylonians of a later period, it can be suggested that among the Cro-Magnons there was a belief that blood was the fountain of life, and that the loss of life could have been due to the loss of the red fluid that flowed through their veins. It would have been noted that strong men who received wounds in battle or with wild animals, were seen to faint or die as a consequence of profuse bleeding. Those who were sick grew ashen pale because, it would seem to them, that the supply of blood was insufficient. Could it be that these early people wished to prolong life, and believed that by using a substance that coloured the person red that they were doing this? When death finally took place isn't it reasonable to assume that if they smeared the whole body with a red substance this would have a vitalising effect on the deceased in an afterlife? It is also possible to believe that the man who once rested in Goat's Cave, being the only burial, was a very important member of the community, perhaps a leader.

It has also been suggested that because so much worked ivory has been recovered from this cave that it may have been the home of a group of people who traded in ivory products. Perhaps this may have been the first Gower 'factory' to be set up on the Peninsula, and the man buried here the first craftsman of Gower? Dr. K.B. Griffiths, in her *Guide to the Archaeology Collection of Swansea Museum*, says that because of these finds, 'We can claim therefore that Paviland cave is the oldest known homestead, workshop and burial site in Wales.'

In all, over 800 implements were found at Paviland Cave, the most interesting of which can be seen at Swansea Museum. However, the bones of the Red Lady were deposited in the Geology Collection at the Oxford University Museum where 'she' now rests in a case.

Long Hole Cave

Cave occupied during the Upper Palaeolithic period
Location: 1.6km west of Port Eynon. (SS 452 851)
Access: Lies near the top of the cliffs

The cave can be reached by either following the coastal path from Port Eynon west towards Worm's Head, or following the path along the top of the cliffs west from Overton. The cave lies near the top of the cliffs on the Overton side of the Long Hole Nature Reserve.

Long Hole Cave is a natural limestone cave, which runs into the hillside above the cliffs west of Port Eynon. Of all the Gower caves Long Hole is the least inspiring because it lacks the breathtaking settings of the other caves. However, unlike Goat's Cave, access is easy. The entrance is a low arch at the base of the rock face and leads into a dark, winding passage about 13m long. It was first excavated in 1861 by Col. E.R. Wood and the results of these excavations played an important role in the history of British archaeology because it proved that man, using flint tools, had lived at the same time as now extinct flora and fauna—a concept that Buckland had failed to grasp over 40 years previously.[17] More work was carried out at Long Hole in 1969 and the environmental evidence confirmed the cave's use by man to a date early in the last glacial period.[18] A few additional worked bone and stone tools were discovered in the cave and are believed to have belonged to the Middle Palaeolithic period 50,000 to 36,000 BC, although colonisation did not begin in earnest until after 36,000 BC. From the finds it is suggested that the cave was used as a small hunting camp, perhaps by hunters in transit.

The sea level was considerably lower than today and there would have been a large level plain at the foot of the cliffs below the cave, which would have made access easy for the game-hunters. Twenty-two flint tools and the bones of fox, wild horse and reindeer have also been recovered from the floor of the cave. Some of these finds can be seen at Swansea Museum; others are lodged at the British Museum in London.

Cat Hole Cave

Cave occupied during the Upper Palaeolithic period
Location: North-west of Parkmill (SS 538 900)
Access: Public footpath

This cave can be approached from the A4118 west of Parkmill, though parking here is difficult. Alternatively you can take the minor road to the north signposted Lunnon and Ilston. Stay on the major of these lanes and shortly after passing through Lunnon you can park in a small lay-by in a dip where a public footpath is sign-posted off to the left up the entrance drive to a house. Follow this well marked and trod path down the valley where it traverses a field, passes round a small waterworks and enters a broad valley. Head onto the track in the middle of the valley, soon passing Parc le Breos burial chamber on the left. The cave is about 50ft up on the right hand side of the valley as it swings round to the left, and is reached by a track and rough steps.

Cat Hole Cave is a natural inland limestone cave occupied during the Palaeolithic and later, and is not difficult to reach. It is situated at the base of a small cliff above the flat floor of a dry lime-stone valley. It has a spacious chamber at its mouth and a small passage running some 18m into the hillside. The twin entrances have a broad open platform—similar to the rocky platform at Paviland—which formed a working area for the early hunters.[19]

It was first occupied in the Early Upper Palaeolithic periods (36,000 to 25,000 BC) and, at this time, was probably used only as a temporary or transit camp, as the earliest flint tools found are associated with Ice Age animal remains. However, most of the stone tools and the waste products discovered belong to the Creswellian period—the Late Upper Palaeolithic (10,000 to 8,000 BC) when the ice cap was beginning to melt. Archaeologists believe that Cat Hole was used on expeditions by the same group which also stayed at Goat's Cave and Long Hole cave.

Finds dating between 8,000 to 4,000 BC show that the cave was again occupied, this time by Mesolithic hunters, the artefacts indicating a more settled occupation. It was again used during the

Bronze Age as a burial chamber, and the finding of medieval pot sherds indicate later use. Isaac Hamon claims that even comparatively recently people were afraid to pass the cave as it was believed to be the hideout of a gang of robbers.

Cat Hole was first excavated by Col. E.R. Wood in 1864, and the earliest finds—flint implements belonging to the Creswellian culture and fauna associated with a cold Palaeolithic period—were recovered. However, these details were not recorded, but a further excavation at the front of the cave by C.B.M. McBurney defined and confirmed the former discoveries.[20] It was also discovered that the natural ditch outside the entrance had been enlarged from about 2m outwards from the cave. In the spoil from this work, amongst fragments of rock, was evidence of a cold fauna including the bones of red fox, Arctic fox, brown bear, Arctic lemming and tundra vole. There was also some evidence of a flint industry. The finds are all at the British Museum.

Several human bones, also preserved at the British Museum, were discovered within the cave by Col. Wood, but are of an uncertain date. A small cave to the north of Cat Hole was excavated sometime before 1887 and found to connect to the main cave. This contained more animal bones, including those of a cave-bear, horse, woolly rhinoceros, mammoth, hyena and reindeer, as well as a portion of a human skull. In 1958, excavation of a Bronze Age layer revealed some scattered human remains and two sherds from burial urns ornamented with cord-impressions, and a bronze socketed axe.

Further investigation in 1964 to 1968 revealed a total of 131 artefacts including a finely polished bone sewing needle, and a flint tool with a tanged point barb, indicating occupation during the Mesolithic when conditions were much warmer.[21]

Minchin Hole

Cave occupied during the Upper Palaeolithic
Location: At the back of a deep recess in the cliffs west of Pwll
Du Head (SS 555 868)
Access: Difficult and requires some scrambling

Minchin, or Mitchin Hole as it is sometimes written is situated in the cliff face, about 600 yards south-south-east of the old Southgate bus terminus, below a small limestone knoll. It is the largest of the coastal caves and can be reached by walking eastward along the shore from Foxhole Bay, which lies just below the car park.

The cave was partly explored in 1850 by Col. E.R. Wood and was the subject of further excavation in 1932 by Mr. T.N. George, when the remains of elephant, bison, soft-nosed rhinoceros and hyena, as well as traces of human occupation were found.[22] It is also one of the few Gower sites where bones of lion have been discovered. Further excavation was carried out by Mr. J.G. Rutter, former Curator of Archaeology at Swansea Museum, who found evidence that the cave had been occupied during part of the Roman period and again in the Dark Ages. Casual finds picked up between 1896 and 1946 included pottery and metal objects of the Iron Age period as well as Samian coarse ware belonging to the first two centuries AD. Excavations between 1946 and 1959 have defined four distinct hearth areas used during the first five centuries AD. Finds have included over 750 pieces of pots, jars, beakers, dishes and bowls From these excavations also came a series of one annular, one coiled and six penannular bronze brooches, as well as a series of finely worked bone spoons. H.N. Savory in *Dark Age Britain*, in a study of the sub-Roman culture in the Severn basin concludes that these finds range from the third to seventh century; Mr. Rutter concluding that this cave had been used by the native people in times of trouble.

Although access to the cave is difficult, those interested in viewing just the finds can see them in comfort at Swansea Museum.

Tooth Cave

Cave occupied during the Palaeolithic period
Location: North-west of Parkmill (SS 532 909)
Access: The cave is easily reached from a public footpath, though
a metal gate prevents access to the cave itself

The cave can be reached by continuing up the valley path from Parc le Breos / Cat Hole Cave, or by walking down the path from Llethrid Bridge on the B4271, though parking here is awkward. The cave is to the east of the valley floor and about 4 m above it, and barred by a metal gate restricting access to cavers. A large tooth-shaped rock hangs in the entrance, so giving the cave its name. It consists of a passage 5.2m long with a mouth 2m wide and 1.4m high. At the far end of this passage glacial blocking was removed in 1961 to reveal a further passage which led to another cave system. The original entrance to this further cave system has yet to be found.

Excavation by J.C. Harvey, R. Morgan and D.P. Webley into one of the deepest parts of the further cave system revealed flint and bones tools, and human remains from the top of the rubble filling.[23] Further discoveries, including pottery, were made in a passage leading on from the first chamber, where they lay in a naturally deposited layer and were heavily calcified.

The finds from the first chamber included a needle, a spatula and a cylindrical bead of bone, as well as two flake knives, a scraper and four flakes of flint, all of the early Bronze Age, and are items associated with the traditional craft of leatherwork. From the passage itself came a scraper and eight flakes of flint, and many sherds of an overhanging rim urn of early type.

The human remains comprised at least eight individuals, probably four adult males, three adult females and a young girl. All were badly fragmented, disarticulated and incomplete. The skull of one individual had been carefully placed together, indicating rearrangement after decomposition, but it was not ascertained whether the bones came from earlier locations, or from within the cave. The disarray of human bones suggests that the cave was used as a ossuary for remains from a local settlement site. These finds can be seen at the National Museum of Wales.

Parc le Breos

Neolithic chambered cairn 4,000 - 3,000 BC
Location: North of A4118 at Parkmill (SS 537 898)
Access: Public footpath

This tomb can be approached from the A4118 west of Parkmill, though parking here is difficult. Alternatively you can take the minor road to the north signposted Lunnon and Ilston. Stay on the major of these lanes and shortly after passing through Lunnon you can park in a small lay-by in a dip where a public footpath is signposted off to the left up the entrance drive to a house. Follow this well marked and trod path down the valley where it traverses a field, passes round a small waterworks and enters a broad valley. Head onto the track in the middle of the valley, soon passing Parc le Breos burial chamber on the left.

Parc Le Breos is the finest and best-preserved chambered long cairn in South Wales. It is also one of the most investigated and was partially restored in 1960-1961. The cairn was only discovered in 1869 when workmen digging for roadstone came across the stones of the central chamber. At this time the whole of the central structure of the cairn was excavated and a plan made by Sir John Lubbock, the man who introduced the word Neolithic into the

English language.[24] At the time Sir John believed the cairn to be circular but in 1937 Professor Glyn Daniel re-excavated the site and discovered it to be an elongated barrow. The present preserved condition of the tomb is the result of the excavation and consolidation of information by Professor Atkinson in 1961. It was established that the tomb belonged to the Severn-Cotswold tradition, lying in the upper part of a limestone valley, in an area that is today almost permanently dry.

The monument is built of local limestone and has a deep concave-sided forecourt at its southern end. Leading into the cairn from the forecourt is a narrow passage edged with upright stones, off which lead four chambers. The bones of the dead were deposited in the chambers, and the disarticulated remains of some 20 to 24 individuals, including three children were found during the 1869 excavation. Some of the bodies may have been buried, exposed or defleshed elsewhere, before being finally buried here. Apart from a few animal bones, only a few sherds of plain, western Neolithic pottery were discovered, including a rim sherd with slight fluting, one of two now at the Ashmolean Museum, Oxford.

The cairn and its main gallery lie due north-south. This has been demonstrated by a local astronomer, Mr. Richard Roberts, who found that by holding a staff at the passage entrance at mid-day local time, the shadow cast was seen to run precisely through the centre of the passage.

Interestingly, the cairn is situated over the course of an underground stream, and a leading water diviner, Capt. Robert Boothby, once wrote that every long barrow he had investigated had an underground stream running its whole length, an opinion that was also shared by Mr. R.A. Smith, the then keeper of antiquities at the British Museum.[25] This theory has not been proven, but in the case of Parc le Breos the masonry with its unusual wavy coursing, especially clear by moonlight, indicates that it could have been built to honour a subterranean water goddess.

Arthur's Stone or Maen Cetti

```
Neolithic chambered cairn
Location: 1km east of Reynoldstown (SS 491 905)
Access: Public footpath
```

Take the minor road from Reynoldston east towards the B4271. After 1km, on the summit, park and take the track almost due north across the brow of the hill and over moor to the north for about 500m to the cairn. The cairn can be seen from the road, as can an O.S. trig pillar which stands to the west of Arthur's Stone.

Maen Cetti, or Arthur's Stone comprises a large double-chambered Neolithic tomb standing in the remnants of a round cairn. It was first excavated by Sir Gardiner Wilkinson in 1870 and was one of the first sites to be protected under the Ancient Monuments Act of 1882.[26]

The capstone is of Old Red Sandstone, a rock that is local to the ridge, and it appears that the ground under the capstone was dug out, and uprights were then inserted into the sides of the chamber to provide support. In all nine uprights remain although the boulder only rests of four. The tomb was then probably completed with a round cairn of loose stones, through it is unlikely that the huge capstone was ever covered over completely. This type of monument, called 'earthfast', was identified by Professor Glyn Daniel in 1950. No human remains have been found to confirm that it is indeed a tomb.

The monument's names refer to the massive capstone. It is first mentioned in a Triad of the sixteenth century, where the raising of the stone is listed as one of the 'three mighty achievements of the Isle of Britain.' Its first record in English was by Edward Lhuyd who noted it as being used by the 'common people', though without noting the purpose. The fame of Arthur's Stone was such that, it is claimed, a platoon of Breton soldiers *en route* from Milford Haven to the battle of Bosworth, made a 60 miles detour in order to pay their respects to the great stone.

Arthur's Stone has generated many legends, which is hardly surprising when you consider that the giant boulder, weighing some 24 tons, is perched precariously on a few upright slabs. Originally the stone measured about 4m x 3m x 2.2m, but part has split off and now lies broken in three pieces to the west. This has led to one legend in which it is claimed that during the sixth century AD, St. David, the patron saint of Wales, fearing a return to Druidism and the worshipping of pagan gods, struck the stone with his staff and split it, thus proving that it was an altar of the false gods. This legend was recorded by Iolo Morganwg around 1800.[27]

There are also numerous legends in Wales associated with King Arthur. One informs us that the king felt a pebble in his shoe when he was passing through Carmarthenshire on his way to the battle of Camlann. He stopped, removed the stone, and threw it as far as he could. It fell, here, on Cefn Bryn, a distance of seven miles!

It is also claimed that, by moonlight, King Arthur is said to be seen riding a white horse along the path besides the tomb. This path, it is claimed by Sir Gardiner Wilkinson, was part of a pillaged stone avenue.[28] The stone was visited in 1907 by the Rev. John Griffiths and Sir Norman Lockyer, who decided that the avenue was oriented toward the May/November sunrise.[29] Interestingly, a more recent researcher, Mr. Richard Roberts, has suggested that Arthur's Stone is central to a much larger astronomical complex with outlying stones, which mark the more important stations of the solar year indicated by notches on the horizon at Rhossili Down.

However with a large number of boulders scattered over the landscape it is possible with the benefit of hindsight to form many different alignments.

It is also said that on Midsummer's Eve the stone goes down to the shores of the Burry Pill estuary for a drink of water. There is even a delightful old custom whereby young girls would test their lover's fidelity. At midnight and under a full moon, the girl would make a cake from barleymeal and honey. This was wetted with milk before being well kneaded on the stone. Then the girl would crawl three times round the stone on all fours. If her young man appeared it proved that he was faithful and intended to marry her; if not he was not true and had no plans to marry her. The girls believed that it was some magical power from within the stone that made their young man appear, whilst local inhabitants claim that if the young man wanted to marry his sweetheart, he would arrange for the girl's mother to inform him of the impending test.

Sweyne's Howes

> Two chambered cairns with only the
> megalithic chambers surviving
> Location: On the eastern slopes of Rhossili Down (SS 421 898)
> Access: To the east of a public footpath along the ridge of
> Rhossili Down

The footpath along the ridge can either be gained from Rhossili at the southern end, or from Llangennith at the northern end of the Down.

The two cairns of Sweyne's Howes, which are clearly visible on the landward slopes beneath the northern peaks of Rhossili Down, are protected from the prevailing winds. They are very poorly preserved, with only the megalithic chambers surviving—the photograph above shows Sweyne's Howes South in the foreground, with the partially fallen capstone of Sweyne's Howe North towards the skyline of Rhossili Down.. The name Sweyne's Howes stems from the name of a legendary Viking warrior from whom the port of Swansea is said to have derived. Howe is the nordic word for mound and it is claimed that Sweyne is buried here, but the cairns predate any Viking invasion. Another theory is that the name derives from 'swine's houses', a reference to the hut-like appearance of the tombs.

Much of the stone has fallen, making their original layout difficult to determine. In addition they have been greatly disturbed and robbed, each now appearing to be elongated with a large inner chamber surrounded by an irregular spread of smaller stones. Nevertheless, both cairns seem to have been oval-shaped and built of local stone.

Sweyne's Howes North is the better preserved of the two. The remains of a chamber opening from the north is clearly a Portal Dolmen because two tall portals still remain *in situ*, with the capstone leaning against the two supporters. The closing slab has fallen backwards and its base is now facing north and out of its socket. A fallen roofing stone also rests against the south side of the portal—there is no trace of any other posts.

Sweyne's Howes South again opens from the north and is probably a Portal Dolmen. Inside the cairn there are a few larger boulders, which seem to have formed the east and west side of a wedged-shaped arrangement. At the north end of the chamber, there is one upright and another slab reclining at an odd angle, and these may have once formed one end of a crescent-shaped forecourt. However, there is no group of visible stones that could be identified as the site of a chamber. A plan, produced by Sir Gardiner Wilkinson, shows the central slab to be more rounded, and it has been suggested that a piece had been removed at one stage for use as a millstone.[30]

Sweyne's Howes North

Nicholaston Long Cairn

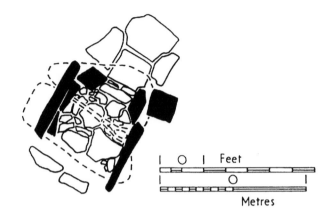

| O | Feet
| O |
Metres

> Poorly preserved chambered cairn
> Location: On the south side of Cefn Bryn (SS 507 888)
> Access: On common land

This poorly preserved chambered long cairn is situated just below the steep southern scarp of Cefn Bryn on the south side of the hill between the hamlet of Perriswoood and Parsonage Farm west of Nicholaston.

It was during quarrying for gravel in 1939 that the capstone was exposed. This led to a thorough excavation by Audrey Williams,[31] and the most prominent feature of the site seen today is the small rectangular chamber which appears as an overgrown feature in the landscape. This is set almost in the centre of a large egg-shaped cairn and is much smaller than most Neolithic tombs, suggesting it was constructed for a single burial rather than the more usual communal one. No human remains were found inside, perhaps because it had been broken into long before excavation took place. The chamber, built of local conglomerate, measured 0.9m by 1.2m, and supported the two stones that formed the roof. There was no evidence of a passage connecting the chamber with the edge of the mound, and access to the chamber was originally from the north-east, across a small area of paving and sill-stone, between two portal upright stones only 0.4m apart. Dry stone walling was used to complete the sides and the whole of the south-west end wall. The latter had been breached at some time, possibly when the contents of the tomb were removed. Fragments of oak and hazel charcoal remained between the internal paving stones.

The cairn consisted of two layers of peaty soil, some with a dominant content of stony fragments, obtained locally and showing signs of fire. Larger stones formed a rough kerb defining the mound.

Penmaen Burrows Chambered Cairn

Crown copyright: RCAHMW

Chambered Cairn of the Severn-Cotswold group
Location: In the sand dunes bordering Threecliff Bay
(SS 532 881)
Access: Difficult to find among the sand dunes

The chambered cairn at Penmaen sits neatly among the sand dunes on a low headland bordering Threecliff Bay. The site was partly exposed in 1893 by the drifting of sands on Penman Burrows. Its original size is unclear as much of the tomb is missing and part is covered in sand, but enough has survived to identify it as being from the Severn-Cotswold group. Two rectangular chambers and an entrance passage are exposed in a hollow below a large dune, and it is assumed that the remainder of the cairn is concealed within the dune.

It appears that the cairn was approached from the east through a passage estimated to be about 2.5m long by 1m high and at least 1m wide between two portal slabs. This opened into a main chamber, approximately 4m long and 2m wide, which was largely covered by

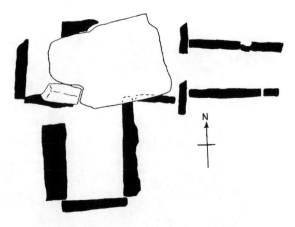

a capstone estimated to weigh about 7 tons. To the south of the
chamber is a transept, and there are indications that there was probably another chamber in the north, so that the tomb originally had
a cruciform plan. Minor excavations were carried out in 1860 by E.
James and M. Moggridge and again in 1881 by Miss Bostock, but
no reports of these excavations have been published. In 1893 the
remains were cleared down to the original ground surface by
William Morgan who did publish a report.[32] Finds were confined to
the south chamber and consisted mainly of a human jaw fragment,
animal bones and a piece of a bone tool handle. Bones were also
noted beneath two paving slabs but were left in place. Three small
pieces of brown pottery of an unknown date were also found on an
early surface.

The Bronze Age

The start of the Age of Metal

By the time the Neolithic had merged into the Bronze Age, around 2000 BC, the inhabitants had domesticated animals and were practising a primitive form of agriculture. They had also learnt to make crude pottery. But the most significant changes in Britain came about with the arrival of another band of people, now called the Beaker Folk, and the advent of the first metal, bronze, which replaced stone as a material for tools and changed the face of the land forever as the Age progressed.

However, despite the age of metal being such an important milestone in the history of Britain, not to mention its effect on man's future development, little is actually known of its early beginnings. It is known that copper was in use in the Near East some two thousand years before it reached the shores of Britain.[33] Here, the natives were content to copy, in flint, those copper items they had seen passing along the ancient trackways and trading routes. For example, at Llanelieu, southern Breconshire, a finely worked pointed oval knife with a square-ended butt made of flint was discovered together with one of the new burial beakers.[34] These objects have now been lost. Closer to West Glamorganshire, a large flint knife was found at Merthyr Mawr Warren.[35] Knives like these are well known from beaker graves in England, but are rare in Wales, and these few isolated examples could possibly represent the beginning of the transition period into the new Age. Early copper items have been found in England and include axes, daggers and awls which, it appears from the quality and design, were imported from other parts of Europe. They were only marginally better than the stone tools used previously for copper is a very soft metal. Before the people of eastern Europe discovered that tin could be added to copper to make bronze, they used arsenic as a hardening ingredient, which presumably lessened the life span of many an early metal worker. (The ideal bronze mix is eight parts copper to one of tin; if too much tin is used the resultant metal shines like silver.)

However, across the sea in Ireland, the story was slightly different. Here, around 2000 BC, the first Irish smiths had began to initiate and master the craft of metal-making, which was to play such a vital role in the foundation of European civilisation. Many like to think that the Bronze Age was marked with the arrival of the slashing sword, such a characteristic object of the Indo-European warriors on the continent. However, in reality it was the development of the industry as a whole and the associated advancement in food production which led to a larger, better equipped and healthier population that heralded the beginning of the Bronze Age.

In Ireland, the copper ore came mainly from the Wicklow Hills and was worked into sheets and shaped and chased with skill by the Irish craftsmen. The interest that would have been generated as news of these fine products travelled along the trading routes can only be imagined. This was an age of no money and goods were bartered or swapped as gifts, each gift possibly entailing an obligation or a repayment of service. This bartering might have included the services of an expert to train their own craftsman, so that in time he would make items to order for the chief and his clan. Perhaps there was competition too as each clan vied with the next, and displayed their 'best' pieces—anyone who wanted to impress would compete to own an ornament or weapon made of bronze, the then status symbol.

One of the routes followed by the Irish trade to southern England and northern France appears to have been along the coast of south Wales, partly by land and partly by the Bristol Channel. The route may well have crossed the Gower Peninsula with a primitive ferry service transporting the traders over Carmarthen and Swansea Bays. This could account for the abundance of Bronze Age settlements on the Gower Peninsula, particularly along Rhossili Down and on the ridge at Cefn Bryn.

Metal became more plentiful once copper was mined in Wales as well as in other parts of Britain and Ireland, and mixed with the tin from the tin mines of Cornwall. It would not have taken long for the people of Britain to develop their own skills in this new craft.

New designs and techniques were being developed and perfected too. The metal smith's workshop become more planned and furnished, and although it is impossible to re-create a true example, we can assume that the craftsman worked at a bench of stone slabs in a round hut with low stone walls. For the actual smelting process he would need heat and this would have been provided by an ordinary domestic fire in the middle of the floor, or an open bowl furnace with charcoal as fuel. We can assume that for high temperature work he would have required a hotter furnace, built into the low wall, with a blast of air being provided by skin bellows and hard work. Near to the furnace would have been a casting pit where a prepared mould was held upright in earth or sand ready to receive the molten metal. Stone shelves would have held stone hammers and the chasing tools ready for the craftsman to use. The sheet bronze would have been hammered into shape to make cauldrons, allowing people for the first time to cook for large numbers at any one time.

Early Bronze Age—The Beakers

The Beaker Folk came from northern and eastern Europe, mostly from Holland and around the Rhine. In Europe they may have integrated with members of the Nordic races, and it is possible that this mixed race of people brought the first elements of the embryonic Celtic culture to Britain. In south Wales they confined themselves mainly to the lower Wye and Usk valleys, the Vale of Glamorganshire, the Gower Peninsula and the south of Carmarthenshire and Pembrokeshire. However, today there is a tendency to think of their arrival not as a massive invasion of people, but as one of ideas, interspersed with small groups of people arriving and settling.

Unlike the Iberians, who were dark-haired, long-headed and short in stature, this new mixed stock race showed elements of the round-headed alpine race and were much taller with fairer hair. They were also more powerful, having descended from the northern warrior peoples and whilst it would be easy for us to think in terms of the big, strong fair men systematically 'conquering' the smaller dark men, in reality many long-headed and round-headed skeletons have been found buried together. This suggests that, some at least, lived harmoniously together and may well have 'inter-married'. These peoples also spoke a sort of Indo-European language and it is now believed they were responsible for introducing a language from which Erse and Gaelic have been developed.

The name Beaker Folk is derived from the high quality bell-shaped collared urns or beakers that are found amongst their valued grave goods. These urns are generally tall, open-mouthed, narrow necked with an S-shaped profile. They are often elaborately decorated with incised patterns made by using a wing bone of a bird as a chisel to mark the wet clay. Others, decorated with multiple chevrons, are more rare. This pottery, distinctive because of its wicker basket decoration, evolved in Spain during the latter part of the Neolithic period — probably from small baskets or vessels made from esparto grass. The ornamental horizontal bands on the pottery are typical of the Spanish 'zone' pots and beakers and are reminiscent of the hoops which formed the framework of the woven model. They may have been used, as the name implies, as a personal drinking vessel to hold barley wine or mead and appear to have been part of the burial ritual. Some clues concerning the contents may be deduced from an excavation in Scotland. An analysis of the pollen grains found in an organic layer of soil in Fife revealed lime pollen which had been spilled from a beaker. Lime flowers are what one would expect to find in a honeyed drink, such as mead, made from fermented lime honey and flavoured with meadowsweet. It has also been suggested that the cord used to decorate beakers was hemp or cannabis which, when combined with the alcohol, would doubtless have produced a potent cocktail! Earlier pottery indicates, by its size, that they were used for the communal consumption of food and drink, and perhaps beakers were the beginning of a period when each individual had his or her own drinking cup. The writer speculates that this may have been introduced because of the perception that some disease or ailment was passed on through using the same vessel. Upon the owner's death the beaker would have been filled with a herb flavoured alcoholic drink, which they believed would help to sustain the deceased on the journey to the next world, and buried with him.

The Beaker Folk had a warlike tradition and were expert archers. Some were armed with polished stone battle axes, and some had a knowledge of and knew the benefits of the new metal — Bronze. Probably a few had actually brought metal tools with them from the continent, but once here, they were quick to exploit the craft of the Irish smiths who, in turn, were only too willing to supply them with objects in bronze. Despite the metal being rare and costly to produce, the idea caught on, not only for utilitarian purposes, but also because the Beaker Folk and the others who adopted their customs liked bright objects and enjoyed wearing ornaments of Irish metal.

By this time the climate was warm with long dry summers, and there was ample grazing land on which people could settle. However, throughout the whole of Britain only a few hut sites have been discovered in comparison with the many burial mounds. Could it be that these first Bronze Age people were in fact more nomadic than their predecessors, with an even more sparse agricultural system, and living mainly in skin and felt tents?

It is hard for us today to paint a true picture but despite their nomadic traits, it can be safely assumed that the Beaker Folk had a highly patriarchal order of society. The male head of the family group was the absolute master of his own woman and children, his bondsmen, his slaves and his herds, though it can be surmised that the woman was able to share on equal terms much of the pastoral work. Her importance as the child bearer was vital to the economy and maintaining the continuity of the tribe. This alone placed a high value on her. Such strong, fertile and skilful women might also have been exchanged for many head of cattle, thus giving them their own status value within the family group.

Life in the Early Bronze Age
From material discovered at the few sites that have been located the early Beaker Folk appear to have relied largely on cattle, pigs, sheep, and wild animals for their food supply. The bulk of information has been amassed from the middens—heaps of accumulated refuse, broken pottery, and implements. These 'kitchen middens'

are especially common on the seashore where they consist chiefly of the remains of edible shellfish. In Gower, ancient middens are in evidence on Worm's Head, at Burry Holms, and along the north-west coast of Llangenydd and Llanmadoc. In the sand dunes between Spritsall Tor and Hills Tor, Llanmadoc, a fragment of a beaker resting in clay, and an elongated pebble were found.[36] No traces of any early shelters have been found, but it is most probable that they were flimsy and any evidence would be very slight and extremely difficult for archaeologists to uncover.

The real Bronze Age in Wales did not begin until after the close of this Beaker period, which must have been viewed by the natives as a mini Industrial Revolution. By this time, around 1500 to 1000 BC, the invention of the wheel and the development of the plough had transformed the landscape forever. As more knowledge was gained, and with better tools and skills man was able to shape the landscape with greater success than with the old Stone Age implements. Early ploughs would have comprised of little more than a forked stick, but gradually more sophisticated tools were developed which would have been pulled by oxen, the yoke being lashed to the animals' horns rather than placed over its shoulders. Studies of the soil indicate that these people had also learnt to use manure and this would have led to increased cereal production. This in turn contributed to an increase in population, more dramatic than at any other time in prehistory because famine would not have been a threat, and healthier women would have produced healthier children which would have helped to reduce the risk of infant deaths.

Whereas Neolithic settlements were centred on the lowlands, with the warmer climate the early Bronze Age people moved into the uplands. People grouped together in small villages and lived in crude, circular huts which were smaller than the Neolithic long houses. They protected themselves against marauders from adjacent villages or from raiders from across the Irish Sea by building a single ditch around the settlement. Like the Neolithic, the discovery of Bronze Age settlements is left very much to chance. However, we do know that caves were also used as dwellings; finds at two caves, Lesser Garth Cave and Culver Hole Cave in Gower, have indicated that they were inhabited during the Bronze Age period.

Cooking Mounds

These mounds mark the positions of cooking-places where meat would have been boiled or roasted. They are generally crescent or horseshoe shaped, with the central hollow opening towards a small stream or pool. The hollow always corresponds with the position on the platform where the fire was lighted. Between the platform and the stream was a sunken trough which was filled with water. The meat was boiled in this trough by casting in hot stones, and the mound was formed by an accumulation of discarded stones, charcoal and burnt earth from the fire due to the continual clearance of the trough and platform after use. The remains are therefore distinctive and unmistakable. There are very few known cooking mounds in the Glamorganshire area, but this could be misleading because, as they consist of a very low shapeless mound, others may have gone, and are still going, unrecognised. In Glamorganshire the mounds range from nearly circular to oval with the length as much as one and a half times the breadth.

Most information relating to the use of these mounds has been recovered from Ireland and, after studying two troughs, Mr. M.J. O'Kelly outlined the possibility of boiling by this method, and obtained a radio-carbon dating of 1553 BC to 1760 BC.[37] Some mounds dating from the Bronze Age have been excavated in Dyfed, but only one has been excavated in Glamorganshire, just outside the area covered by this book, in Raydr (ST 134 800). A shapeless oval mound at the foot of a steep slope, it is now landscaped into an amenity area so could easily be missed. The mound is composed of burnt stones, charcoal and black earth, some of which is still visible on the surface, with a stream running along its west side. It was excavated in 1916 when pottery fragments indicated occupation during or before the first century AD. No animal bones were found around the mound which suggests that the cooked food was eaten elsewhere. Interestingly, all the species of trees which currently grow in the woods that surround the site have been identified in the charcoal in the mound, with the exception of birch.

No other Glamorganshire mounds have been excavated, although there are two Gower sites—Druids Moor south of Harding's Down (SS 438 899), and another near Nicholaston (SS 513 887)—that has surface disturbance exposing a typical mixture of burnt and broken stones mixed with blackened earth and charcoal.

Funerary Customs

During the Bronze Age major changes in the way people were buried occurred, although some of these changes had already started to come about towards the end of the Neolithic period. Instead of placing their dead in large stone communal chambered tombs, they began to use a much wider range of monument. Unlike the previous Age, the dead were buried singly in stone cists or coffins, often covered with a mound or earth as a barrow. The barrow varied in design, sometimes with and sometimes without kerbstones, sometimes surrounded by a ditch or circular arrangement of stones. The body was usually placed on its side in a crouching position, and buried either in a stone-lined cist or sometimes without the stones. Alongside was placed the distinctive beaker, and sometimes ornaments and weapons indicating wealth. The burial of people singly points to a developing hierarchical social structure which was to develop into a highly privileged aristocratic class in the Iron Age. No complete beakers have been found in tombs in West Glamorganshire, although a few fragments were recovered not far away at Merthyr Mawr Warren near Porthcawl.

With such little evidence of settlements, it is to the barrows and single round cairns that we have to look for information about lifestyle during this period, together with caves that were used for burials, especially those along the Gower coastline—Culver Hole, Tooth Cave, Cat Hole and Lesser Garth Cave.

Some 400 barrows and single round cairns have been found dotted about the Glamorganshire landscape. The total for this area far exceeds that of any other type of prehistoric structure, but to interpret these figures as indicating a highly populated area would be misleading, for these burials took place over a period of several centuries. Many lay undiscovered until the mound was ploughed through by a farmer or, in a much later age, when a mechanical excavator was used to prepare land for another use. Sadly none of these monuments survive in their original state as most have suffered from plough damage, the passage of time and stone and grave robbing. Yet, the known cairns can hardly be representative of the number of people who lived and died during this period. Either several of these burial sites have been destroyed or lost without trace, or it is likely that only the aristocracy, the Beaker chiefs, their women and children, as well as a handful of important members of society were so buried, and the rest disposed of in some other way.

Between Merthyr Mawr and Porthcawl lies Riley's Tumulus (SS 850 770), a large mound, in which six skeletons were unearthed. Two were of children, and four of men whose height ranged from 5ft 1in to about 5ft 7in all with rounded skulls, typical of the beaker-folk in general. Many other Bronze Age objects were recorded, but the constant movement of sand makes the identification of sites such as these difficult. This site was first investigated in 1904 by W. Riley, after whom it is named. In 1919 J. Ward attempted to record the discoveries, but it was clear from the report that they had to rely on confusing and unreliable verbal information. For example, the burial mound was said to be 54ft in length and 21ft high, although a sketch of the work in progress suggests that the height was greatly exaggerated.[38] At the site two stone cists were revealed. The larger contained the crouched skeleton of a man, his head resting on one side and supported on a stone pillow. The other cist contained the crouched skeletons of two children facing each other. On the north side of the mound were three other burials without cists. The crouched skeleton of one man, lying on the right with his head facing to the north-north-west had a small piece of flint near his shoulder and a distinctive beaker. The flexed skeleton of another man lying on his back with his legs turned to the right, had several long bones broken. Near the head, which again rested on a stone pillow, was a beaker, which can now been seen at Swansea Museum. The flexed skeleton of yet another man had a scattering of charcoal over the body, and near the feet was a beaker.[39] In 1948 A.H. Roberts and H.N. Savory examined another burial mound (SS 859 770) and found a cist containing the crouched skeleton of a child, and to the south, a set of stones forming a segment of a circle. Two kerbs near the circle contained fragments of burnt and unburnt bones, which may have been the remains of yet another cist.[40] In 1953 small fragments of a cinerary urn, a flint scraper and a barbed and tanged arrowhead were also found in the vicinity of the earlier finds.[41] The beaker pottery was the subject of a full and careful study by D.L. Clarke, *Beaker Pottery of Great Britain and Ireland*, in 1970. In his book Clarke dates the finds at the Merthyr Mawr sites to within a period of 1700 to 1475 BC.

The barrows in the Glamorganshire area are located mainly in the upland ridges and usually in prominent positions. Some are so large that they could almost be termed cemeteries. Others have several cists, often near the surface. Many were uncovered during the Second World War when new aerodromes were being hastily built to help the war effort. An equally hasty archaeology programme followed under the direction Sir Cyril Fox, then keeper of archaeology at the National Museum of Wales. During these excavations the barrows were often found not just to be a mere mound of earth covering a burial, but the final stage of a complex ritual site with entrances blocked and the site enclosed with stakes or stones which had been laid out on the ground surface. This had been followed by the burial in a stone cist, and with the earlier bodies rested in a crouched position. The weapons buried with the corpse had been deliberately broken, either to release spirits or to prevent the living using the deceased's personal property. There is evidence of feasting and of fires following the burial ceremony, and pits were dug either to release evil spirits, or as a receptacle to hold an offering to the earth spirit.

Another tomb variant is the ring cairn. Here, instead of a mound, a circular bank surrounds a level area in which there is usually a sunken stone-lined burial or cist. A circle of upright stones may replace the bank as in the case of the Carn Llechart stone circle at Pontardawe, and the cairn circle on Rhossili Down on the Gower Peninsula.

Whichever method was used it is clear that Bronze Age man had a well-developed system of burial. The majority of round barrows in West Glamorganshire are situated just below the highest areas of the hills and ridges. On the Gower Peninsula they are almost completely restricted to the Old Red Sandstone hills, and in the remainder of West Glamorganshire to the Pennant Grit ridges. These elevated areas are agriculturally poor and offer little or no rough grazing, which may be a reason why they were chosen for burial sites.

The only round barrows in West Glamorganshire to be investigated in recent times are two of the few earthen mounds that have been placed on the lowlands. These barrows, Pennard Burch and Bishopston Burch, were situated on Fairwood Common in the eastern half of the Gower Peninsula and were excavated by Mrs. Audrey Williams in 1941, prior to their destruction during the construction of Swansea Airfield.[42]

Pennard Burch measured 27.4m in diameter and had been first opened sometime before 1855 by Lady Mary Cole, when fragments of an overhanging rim urn were found, but not recorded. Audrey Williams found a slight trace of a stone cist. However, the primary burial had been rifled by early excavators, though evidence of a pyre of oak branches, which had been burnt over the cist after burial and then covered by a small stone cairn, was also revealed. These fragments represented the only burial, which had been placed in a slight hollow under a heap of stones and covered with a mound built in five stages—a pile of grey clay, then a cairn ring, infilled with a turf mound, followed by a mound of brown clay and ending with a stone kerb near the perimeter. Obviously there was some reason for this elaborate construction, but as yet, it remains a mystery to modern man.

Bishopston Burch (SS 571 909) was a simpler structure than Pennard Burch. It measured approximately 9m in diameter, and again this site had been broken into and severely damaged during the nineteenth century. In 1941 workmen erecting an Ordnance Survey station uncovered a cinerary urn, and this lead to an excavation by Mrs. Audrey Williams. The barrow included a central burial pit, in which a collared urn containing the remains of a child of 10-14 years of age was found. After the burial the pit had been filled with small stones and a scatter of oak and hazel charcoal. Over the pit was a cairn covered by a mound of clay and turves. Within and under the cairn were fragments of four overhanging rim urns from secondary burials. Fragments of pottery found during this excavation are now at Swansea Museum.[43]

Another site forever lost to modern man is Colts Hill, on enclosed land near Oystermouth Castle (SS 605 887). It was first excavated in 1929 by A.L. Jones and was described as being a circular mound of earth and stones, 15m in diameter, covering a buried ring of piled boulders.[44] In the centre was a shallow pit and against the inner side of the boulder wall were the remains of three cists. No other finds were discovered. However, when it was re-examined in 1968 it was found to consist of a square mound, much overgrown and covered in thorn and bracken and it was clear that the mound had been trimmed from its original form. H.N. Savory re-excavated the site in 1969, prior to its destruction for housing development, and found that it consisted of a core of sandy loam covered with a casing of beach pebbles. The primary burial lay in a pit slightly to the north-west of the centre and was filled with loose stones mixed with fragments of burnt human bone. Near the pit were found the crushed fragments of a food vessel and scattered fragments of Beaker pottery, whilst a ring of post-holes under the cairn indicated it had been built on the site of a circular hut about 9m in diameter. There was also evidence of a hearth, and sherds of a later variety of beaker ware. The burial would seem to have occurred on top of an early settlement.[45]

The Middle Bronze Age—1450-1000 BC

By the middle Bronze Age there seemed to be a unification and gradual development of the Beaker and Neolithic races into a common culture. Inhumation slowly gave way to cremation, the ashes of the dead being emptied into a leather bag or an ornamental earthenware urn or vase prior to burial, the drinking vessel being abandoned in favour of these large cinerary urns. These urns were sometimes placed in an inverted position and usually protected by a stone coffin covered with a mound of earth.

Cinerary urns from Carn Goch

Frequently these large urns were accompanied by a small 'incense cup' or a pigmy vessel. These pots rarely show signs of having been burnt with the cremation, and their purpose is unknown. It has been argued that they were ritual containers for the ceremonial flame with which the funeral pyre had been ignited. Pigmy cups are usually less than three inches in height, with no handles but having holes in opposite pairs or in fours, near the bottom as well as the top of the pot, making it unlikely that they were used for holding liquids.

*'Incense cup' from
Carn Goch*

The only such cups to be uncovered in West Glamorganshire were at Carn Goch common, east of Loughor on the B4620. Less than a kilometre from Carn Goch Hospital is a much damaged Bronze Age mound which can be seen from the roadside (SS 605 980). The destruction of this site began in 1800 when the topmost layer of stones were robbed for road building, and what remained of the mound was dug up in 1855 by J.T.D. Llewelyn. Beneath the mound of earth Llewelyn found a ring cairn with a burial cist placed off-centre. Nine funerary urns with human remains were found within the ring, along with two pigmy cups and two flint implements, a knife and a spearhead. Some of the urns and one of the pigmy cups are now in the British Museum, whilst another urn is at Swansea Museum. Unfortunately much of the evidence from this site has been destroyed so it is difficult to establish whether the internal structure contained work from more than one period. Re-excavation at some future date may clarify the mystery of Carn Goch. Other pigmy cups have been found outside the area at Cowbridge and Templeton in Pembrokeshire.

In Wales the commonest form of cinerary urns are the overhanging rim type. The earliest have been found in southern England, but several examples of early urns have also been discovered on Fairwood Common, Llanmadoc Hill and again at the Carn Coch site.

During the Middle to Late Bronze Age it is generally believed that several small bands of settlers filtered into Britain, followed by ever increasing numbers. This gave rise to a number of new traditions, and their originators were given the collective cultural name of Deverel-Rimbury Folk (after two Dorset sites, a barrow and a cemetery). The term has since been loosely applied and linked to the pottery and burial customs of these people. It is suggested that this particular group of people arrived in Britain from the Lower Rhine region and occupied the area that later became known as Wessex. They integrated well with the inhabitants of Britain and helped to develop a common culture—the Wessex culture—which included the use of round, bucket or barrel shape urns, and the creation of large cemeteries or urnfields. Gradually the influence of the Deverel-Rimbury culture spread, eventually reaching as far as south Wales. Lesser Garth Cave (ST 125 821), situated outside the area covered in this book on the south-east corner of Garth Hill overlooking the Taf Gorge has revealed some interesting finds. Two excavations in 1912, one by T.E. Lewis and another by R.E.M. Wheeler yielded finds of Bronze Age pottery and human remains. Further excavations in 1963-4 revealed a series of ten bucket-like urns in the Wessex urn tradition.[46]

Culver Hole in Llangenydd (SS 405 929) has also revealed pottery from the same period. It was first excavated in 1924 by H.E. David and the remains of eleven individuals were uncovered. Further excavations in 1931 by R.G. Dingwall and then by T.K. Perriman and Lord Forrester recovered the skeletons of at least 30 individuals of a wide range of physical types, together with pottery which made up some eleven bucket-like urns contemporary with the Deverel-Rimbury Middle Bronze Age period.[47] Further excavation at Culver Hole showed that it was indeed inhabited in the Middle Bronze Age period and that people built hearths and left a large quantity of animal bones—oxen, pigs and sheep or goats as well as fragments of domestic pottery. The pottery consisted of barrel-shaped pots, some fine and some much coarser and decorated with finger-printed cordons on the rim and shoulder. A small cylindrical pot had been decorated with small, unpierced bosses linked to the Deverel-Rimbury group in Southern England.

Climatic Changes
During the Middle Bronze Age the climate became much colder and wetter and by 1200 BC much of the upland areas had turned into bogs. A theory that is currently being investigated is that in

1159 BC, Hekla, a volcano off the coast of Iceland, erupted and sent tons of dust into the atmosphere. According to some archaeologists this would have created the Bronze Age equivalent of a 'nuclear' winter—a dense cloud of volcanic ash blocking out the sun's rays as it gradually settled over the landscape. It would have caused the climate to worsen and harvests to fail with the result that people living in affected areas would have been forced to move or starve. Whilst archaeologists have found evidence of volcanic fallout in western and northern Scotland, other recent research suggests that the climate was not severely altered by the eruption.[48] However, the eruption apparently caused large quantities of sulphur to be emitted into the air and this fell to earth as acid rain between 1158 and 1153 BC. Settlements on acid soil were doomed, crops would have failed and animals would have contracted a rotting disease known as *flurosis*. This theory does not, however, explain why the chalk uplands in the south were also deserted—perhaps there were other more far reaching factors at work.

Cultural changes at work
Whatever it was that brought about these shifts, they probably instigated cultural changes. For some reason burials in single cairns and barrows ceased and small groups of cairns took their place. These groups were first recognised in Glamorganshire by Sir Cyril and Lady Fox, who described their general features and published, in May 1935, a list of six—all outside the area of this book. They added a further four in November of that year and four more the following November. Two of these are within the scope of this book. One is on the ridge above the Gwenffrywd stream to the east of Tonna (SS 803 992) where Lady Fox recorded at least 36 cairns scattered over a distance of more than 400m. The other, near Penrhiw Angharad, east of Tonna (SS 799 991) comprised six mounds and a curving section of bank, all built of small stones.[49] In the same year they excavated two platform houses on the western side of Gelli-gaer Common and noted an adjacent cairn.[50] In July 1941 Lady Fox and M.E. Murray Threipland decided to undertake a systematic excavation of two groups, whilst listing a total of 16 assemblages of this type in the Glamorganshire area.[51]

At the first site, Llwyncelyn, near Rhigos Halt (SN 932 066) ten cairns were recorded, of which eight were circular and two were oval. Five were excavated and all proved to be built of small stones. All had been robbed but three had small central hollows, possibly the remains of the actual graves. Today the site lies on a derelict portion of an industrial site.

The other site, at Twyn Bryn-hir near Rhigos sewage farm (centred at SN 377 066) is at the edge of ground that falls away to the north. 17 mounds were found in an area extending 165m from east to west and 69m north to south. 12 were excavated by Lady Fox and M.E. Murray Threipland, none revealing any signs of burial or grave goods, although two contained four slabs which might have been the remains of disturbed cists. Another mound covered a rectangular hole and was floored with a flat slab, whilst four others were termed as 'scoop-graves', although no remains were found. It was surmised that the turf was removed and the body laid in shallow scoop so formed, that stones were then placed around the head and body and the whole then covered with soil dug from ditches around the grave. Finally the mound would have been bordered and perhaps covered with stones gathered from round the site.

Lady Fox wrote, 'We are frankly puzzled at the complete absence of any trace of human remains, for not a piece of charcoal or cremated bone occurred in any of the cairns investigated.' What does this mean? Were these mounds burial mounds or not? Investigations in other parts of the country since the Second World War have done little to provide a clear cut answer, but have tended to lessen rather than increase confidence that the mounds were used for sepulchral purposes. In 1950 W.E. Griffiths excavated six cairns in a large cemetery on the eastern slopes of Penmaenmawr in Caernarvonshire and proved that, on this site at least, all the features were consistent with burial, in that they had an internal kerbing and upright stones.[52] One of the cairns overlay some fragments belonging to the Romano-British period indicating that the cairn was of much later than Bronze Age date, indicating a reversion to older practices. The most likely explanation of lack of evidence as cemetery sites could be that the inhabitants of the Iron Age cleared the area around for cultivation, the cairns being the spoil heaps. However there are some sites, such as the group of cairns at Cefn Bryn on the Gower Peninsula, that were probably cemetery sites.

Ceremonial Monuments—Stone Circles and Standing Stones

Other changes were also occurring. New ceremonial monuments, such as henges and stone circles were beginning to be erected. Aubrey Burl and others have argued that Stone Circles erected during the Bronze Age are purely a British innovation, though this theory has been challenged in recent years and archaeologists now tend to think of stone circles as part of a 'cultural package'.[53] When stone circles are looked at in detail, most are seen to have been built during the period 2500-1600 BC—the Early and Middle Bronze Age. It is thought that the development of these stone circles began towards the end of the Neolithic with the circular kerbing around passage graves (such as Bryn Celli Ddu on the Isle of Anglesey in north Wales).

The stone circles found in Wales are small—in number as well as in stature—and represent only five per cent of those found in Britain. Their exact purpose is still unknown, but it appears that the influences on stone circles in Wales may have derived from Ireland and Scotland. A merging of customs can be seen, especially in places like Carn Llechart, where the traditional ring cairns of the Neolithic and the free standing circles of the Bronze Age come together. Here, the central cist or burial mound is surrounded by a stone circle about 60ft in diameter. Whilst Neolithic peoples appear to have held ceremonies in the forecourts of the burial chambers, it appears Bronze Age people held their religious meetings in or around ceremonial stone circles. This site offers a combination of both. Unlike the Neolithic people who worshipped the earth, it is believed that Bronze Age people believed in a sky god, possibly the sun. This may be one of the reasons why stone circles are sited on high ground, so that they could be nearer to their god. The change from earth to sun god could also have occurred because of the climatic changes. No longer could the people rely on the earth god to provide a good harvest, and as famine was always a major problem to society they would need to look elsewhere for help and guidance.

The Maen Hir, or standing stones, as well as the stone circles were part of the ceremonies that formed such a vital part of the

Bronze Age tribal life. A remarkable number of standing stones have been recorded in the Royal Commission on Ancient and Historical Monuments inventory, although less than 20 survive in Glamorganshire. Only eleven of these are considered to genuinely date to the Bronze Age, but if field name evidence and documented lost sites are added to the list the number rises again to be in excess of 30. Although no stone circles exist in Gower today there is a remarkable concentration of standing stones in western Gower; all situated away from the high downs occupied by the cairns. Apart from this their distribution appears to be totally random. Areas around three of the standing stones have been excavated. The groups of standing stones at Burry and St Nicholas (ST 080 741) produced no results, whilst the third, near Bridgend (SS 902 795), was found to be associated with an undated cremation. The excavator, J.M. Lewis, was of the opinion that the cremation was a dedicatory deposit intended to venerate the stone.[54]

Carreg Bica

Archaeological evidence points to no single function for the setting up of these stones. Some were gravestones, others may have been boundary markers, shrines or commemorative stones. However, most of those in the Gower area would appear to be the only visible permanent object of a much larger ritual site and could possibly have been linked to more elaborate stone circles that have since been destroyed. Looking at the evidence as a whole it seems likely that most of the standing stones were erected in the Bronze Age and are therefore contemporary with the round cairns.

Some people assume that, in part at least, both the stone circles and individual standing stones were related to major events, such as the changing of the seasons, the movements of heavenly bodies, or the rising and setting of the sun and moon. Perhaps these circles were an astronomical clock, laid out with such exactness that skilled practitioners could, by noting the position of the sun, moon and stars, acquire knowledge of seasons or gain information about the stars to use as directions when travelling. We can only guess the power that one Bronze Age man would have achieved by correctly predicting that an eclipse would occur and the day would momentary go black, or that by travelling in accordance with the stars people would reach their desired destination. As such, these standing stones, in time, may provide us with some insight into the minds of the people of the Bronze Age.

The Late Bronze Age
During the Late Bronze Age, traders and immigrants introduced new types of weapons, whilst the development of the old 'native' styles produced several distinctive patterns. These new types included the leaf-shaped sword which is a heavy cutting sword that replaced the thin thrusting sword or rapier, the winged axe, and the socketed axe, as well as the riveted spearhead. One isolated find of an axe came from the Llanmadoc area of Gower, and Evans noted that it is of Scandinavian or North German origin.[55]

A considerable number of bronze tools and weapons have been discovered in 'hoards'—groups of objects deposited together and usually buried in the ground. By far the greatest number of Bronze Age hoards belong to the last phase of the Bronze Age and suggest a huge advancement in the metal industry from 1000 BC onwards.

As metal goods were greatly valued, it could be that they were buried during a time of danger and, for some reason, not recovered by their owner. Over the years archaeologists have speculated why this should be. Some, they claim, were unable to recover them because they had died or perhaps been killed in battle, whilst others may have simply forgotten where they had hidden them. But does this account for all the hoards? Another suggestion put forward is that maybe these hoards had been offered to the forces of earth and water. Perhaps by giving away such items people could increase their honour and prestige within the tribe. Or perhaps they were gifts which signified the bonding of a relationship such as a 'marriage', or signalled the end of a relationship by a parting or death and in doing so the objects were destroyed. One thing is certain, the ideas can be discussed at length, but there are, as yet, no correct answers.

Hoards are, however, sparsely distributed in Wales with only one, the Langrove Hoard at Pennard, found in the west Glamorganshire area. Here, when quarrymen were breaking new ground in 1827, Late Bronze Age weapons were found concealed under a thin, flat stone, in a hole three feet below the surface of the ground, three-quarters of a mile north of Pennard Church. The hoard consisted of three leaf-shaped swords, a spearhead, a socketed axe and a barbed and tanged arrowhead, all made of bronze.

The axe is unusual as it has a square appearance which, although modified by a slight structural ridge in the middle of each side, could indicate that it was made in southern England or even in France. The arrowhead, being of bronze, is extremely rare as normally in north-west Europe these were made from flint. This example is almost certainly of continental origin and is the only one to have been found in Wales. Most of

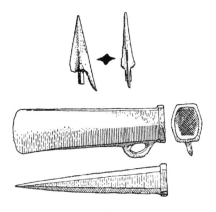

Pieces from the Bronze hoard at Langrove, Gower

Sword found at
Oystermouth
in 1979

the remainder of the hoard is of scrap metal and therefore can give no indication whether there was a bronze industry locally. Another recent find, in 1979, is a complete sword from the old land surface of Swansea Bay, opposite Oystermouth Castle.

Amongst the innovations of the Late Bronze Age was the introduction from the continent of various types of razor and tweezer. These indicate that our ancestors were beginning to take an interest in their appearance. However, only three specimens have been recorded in Wales, one of which, a double leaf type bronze tweezer, found at Llangwyllog in Anglesey is thought to have been used for plucking hair.[56] Another extremely rare find at Llyn Fawr, Glamorganshire, is a crescent-shaped type tweezer probably from the continent and of the type found in the Hallstatt Period, named after the Celtic races who came from Hallstatt in the Austrian Alps.

Another metal in use during the Bronze Age was gold. This was exported from County Wicklow in Ireland not only to Britain but also to the continent, particularly to Denmark and France. Finds of Early Iron Age gold objects are rarer, which suggests that the supply of gold was beginning to run out. Gold was mined in Wales from the time of the Romans, but there is no evidence to show that it was mined during the Bronze Age. Of the few gold items found in Wales of pre-Roman times, it is generally accepted that all were imported.

Gold torcs were in use during the late Bronze Age period but only four or possibly five have come to light in Wales. Some were wound spirally, for use as armlets, whilst others were wound too awkwardly to have been worn comfortably as personal ornaments. The only one found nearest to our area was discovered on the border of Glamorganshire and Breconshire in 1838 and is now in the British Museum.[57] Another is said to have been discovered in a mound 'somewhere between Cowbridge and Bridgend' and is reputed to have been melted down by a Cardiff jeweller! Their purpose is not clear but it has been suggested that they may have been used as girdles for large wooden idols, or to protect the wearer from evil spirits in times of need. It has also been suggested that, as they were circular, they were a symbol of infinity, of the never-ending cycle of death and rebirth.

We know that the Iron Age did not start overnight, nor did the manufacture of Bronze implements stop, and the Llyn Fawr site could well be one of these transition sites as finds of both bronze and iron were discovered. This transition may have started as early as 1000 BC and could have taken as long as half a millennium before the change over was complete. It would have begun with a few prestigious items until, finally, the ordinary tools of the day were made from iron.

Ring Cairns, Rhossili Down

A Group of Bronze Age ring cairns
Location: On Rhossili Down (Most notable SS 421 897)
Access: Alongside public footpaths

Take the B4247 to Rhossili. From the end of a minor road north of church the public footpath leads over Rhossili Down. The cairns are just past the summit, on right hand side of the path. The footpath can also be reached from the northern end of the Down at Llangennith.

Today Rhossili Down is the haunt of the rambler, hang glider and pony trekker, but in Bronze Age times it was the burial site of the aristocracy of Gower, in around 2000 - 1000BC. Around a dozen or more cairns can be seen dotted along the ridge and the eastern slopes on a site known as The Beacon—the photograph above looks across one robbed out cairn to Worm's Head. Most are the usual style of ring cairn formed from local stones, but there are one or two uncommon forms. One (SS 421 897), near Sweyne's Howes on the eastern slope of Rhossili Down, comprises of a circle of upright stones which surrounds a level platform about 0.3m high. The north-western half of the ring is fairly well preserved, but the south-eastern half is virtually destroyed. Many of the stones protrude above the level of the platform, which suggests that they may have originally supported an earth or stone-filled rim. In the middle of the platform is a small hollow, which may be all that remains of a burial cist. It was excavated in 1870 by Sir Gardiner Wilkinson who found charcoal and calcined bones in a cinerary urn, two sherds from which are now in Swansea Museum.[58]

Another cairn or cairn circle, consisting of a heather-clad platform with a kerb of orthostats is located at SS 420 890. A little above the platform are uncertain traces of a possible inner line, suggesting that the platform may have once had a raised rim. A small hollow a little to the south of the centre is possibly the site of a robbed cist.

A third interesting cairn (SS 418 900) is to be found on the south side of an area of the Down called Bessie's Meadow. It consists of a single layer of medium sized boulders with traces of a kerb. Three large blocks at the centre may be the remains of a cist. The cairn lies on the line of the south wall of the meadow which it is presumed was built from material removed from the cairn.

Other cairns on the Down are worth a visit, although little of importance has been recovered from them.

Robbed Cairns, Llanmadoc Hill

> A group of much robbed Bronze Age Cairns
> Location: Llanmadoc Hill (SS 430 927 and SS 440 927)
> Access: By public footpaths; the site can be overgrown with
> gorse and bracken in summer

Several paths lead from Llanmadoc village green to Llanmadoc Hill, which is worth the climb even if only to see the entire length of the Gower Peninsula from the top.

Thanks to the Bronze Age passion for elevated burial sites Llanmadoc Hill is covered with round cairns. In 1867 Davies and O'Donovan counted 19 but more recently the Royal Commission for Ancient and Historical Monuments in Wales could only account for 14.[59] They range from large mounds to small, almost indistinguishable lumps.

Some of the cairns were excavated in 1868, including one located at SS 430 927. A cist was clearly identified, but had been greatly disturbed and only pieces of charcoal were recovered. From another cairn, excavated at the same time, came fragments of at least three cinerary urns, one perhaps being a large food vessel.[60] This cairn lies on the north side of the hill about 250m below the crest of the ridge overlooking the splendour of Broughton Bay. The outline and dimensions are difficult to see because of the extent of robbing and, dependant upon the time of year, the heavy growth of bracken. The covering mound has long been destroyed but a slab-lined burial cist is exposed, slightly to the east of the centre.

However, it is the Great Cairn on the summit (SS 440 927) measuring 27m across that is the most notable. It has been severely robbed, almost down to ground level, but a considerably amount of the cairn material still survives in the north-eastern half and around the centre. Blocks of red sandstone were used to build this mound, and when it was finished it must have been a spectacular sight on the horizon.

There are many other cairns on the hill, but most are difficult to locate owing to the bracken and to the robbing of materials.

Round Cairns, Cefn Bryn

Bronze Age Group of round cairns
Location: 1km east of Reynoldston, near Arthur's Stone
(SS 490 906, SS 492 902, 493 903)
Access: By public footpath

Take the minor road from Reynoldston east towards the B4271. After 1km, on the summit, park and take the track to the north across the brow of the hill and over moor to the north for about 500m to the cairn.

During the Bronze Age the area around Maen Cetti, Arthur's Stone, was extensively used for funerary rites and burials. Over 60 cairns are within a small area east and west of the Stone, although during the summer months they are difficult to find due to a dense covering of undergrowth. Some are likely to be genuine burial sites, others could well be heaps of stones cleared off the land for agricultural use. Two sites have been classed as 'ritual rings'. One lies about 300m south east of the stone and could be the remains of a ring cairn. The other is difficult to find in the undergrowth 150m to the north-east and consists of a long, low mound inside a ring ditch about 30m across. Alongside a faint path which leads east from Arthur's Stone is a group of about half a dozen boulders spaced regularly over a distance of about 100m, and in a rough east / west alignment. During the nineteenth century these were thought to be a rare stone avenue, like the ritual monuments more often found in Cornwall and Devon but, as there are so many natural rocks scattered over Cefn Bryn, it is now considered the alignment is a natural formation.

More prominent on the landscape are the three cairns located north and west of Arthur's Stone that were excavated between 1981 and 1984 by Mr. Anthony Ward.[61] The largest, the Great Cairn, is a saucer-shaped mound of stones raised over a central grave pit. It is most imposing as it stands on a natural rock knoll. Excavation uncovered earlier activity on the site, possibly associated with a late Neolithic settlement, whilst a hollow was discovered on the east side of the chamber. This is believed to be a disturbance caused by Sir Gardiner Wilkinson who reckoned that there were well over a hundred cairns on Cefn Bryn, including a cairn cemetery of 50 small cairns.[62] On the slopes of the north side of the ridge are two ring cairns, the larger having a single entrance gap and an inner ring of kerb stones. The space within the enclosure bank was filled with stones at a later date, either as part of a ritual, or to prevent further ceremonies taking place there.

Samson's Jack & Ty'r-coed Standing Stones

Standing Stones
Location: Near Llanrhidian (Samson's Jack SS 476 926;
Ty'r-coed SS 475 917)
Access: Samson's Jack stands by the side of a public footpath;
Ty'r-coed on private land

Take the minor road west from Llanrhidian. At Oldwalls keep left and continue to the first farm on the right hand side. Park on the verge near here. Take the public footpath to the left of the farm and which follows the field boundary on your left. Samson's Jack is in the hedgerow on your left, near the junction with the second hedgerow of the fields through which you've been walking

Samson's Jack is one of a group of eight standing stones scattered below the western end of Cefn Bryn ridge (also see the Burry Group of Stones) and is the largest standing stone in Gower at 3.2m high. Its odd name may be connected with the sixth century St Samson who, it is claimed, carved a cross on a Cornish standing stone to end its use as a pagan site. It has roughly vertical sides rising to a blunt top and, like the others, is of quartz conglomerate. Samson's Jack points to the mid-winter sunrise, a quality it shares with the Ty'r-coed Stone close by. This menhir stands behind the barn of Ty'r-coed farm and is not accessible to the public, though if you ask at the farmhouse you may gain permission to view it.

Two other standing stones (SS 484 919 and 486 920) sit a little to the east of this stone in the Oldwalls area. Although again neither is accessible to the public they can clearly be seen from the roadside, both set in hedgerows. The first stands 2.2m high just southwest of Pitton Cottage, whilst the other is in a field to the north of the Greyhound Inn.

Burry Menhir, Burry lesser & Burry Standing Stones

Standing Stones
Location: North of Knelston. Burry Menhir, (SS 464 901), the lesser standing stone (SS 463 901), Burry Standing Stone (SS 468 892)
Access: By public footpaths

All can be reached along public paths, either from the south or from the north along a network of footpaths.

The Burry Standing Stone (lower left photograph) is closer to the roads to its south, though parking is difficult. Park in Knelston and take the public footpath which starts along the approach lane to Knelston Hall Farm, itself about 100 yards to the west of the school. Follow the path ahead, and then to the right in front of some farm buildings, passing out into a field at their far end. Follow the track to the left and the stone is near the gate in the next field.

From the north, park near Burry Farm, which lies at the junction of a no through road and the road between Burry Green and Llanddewi. To avoid the farmers at Burry Farm having too many people walking close to their house, walk up the no through road, and cross the stile on your right at the sharp bend you soon reach. Follow the hedge on your left to another stile, crossing this into the

field beyond. If you take the footpath along the hedgerow on your left you'll soon come to the Burry Menhir (top left photograph), and this footpath can be followed to the Burry Standing Stone near Knelston. If you take the footpath alongside the hedge on your right, you'll soon come to the lesser standing stone (photograph this page).

The Burry Group of standing stones, as they are known, are of considerable interest. The Burry Menhir, now lying near the hedge close to the path, would have stood 3m high. After it fell during the severe winter of 1947, Dr. H.N. Savory and J.G. Rutter excavated the hole and found cobble stones had been used as packing around the base, though some modern glass was embedded well down within the packing. There was no sign of a burial or anything to indicate a date of erection.[63] It is said that the stone is one of three, and certainly an old estate map dated 1784, preserved at the National Library of Wales at Aberystwyth, shows three stones and is accurate concerning most of the other features in the landscape, including field gates and hedgerows. To the extreme south-south-east of the Menhir, in a hedge, is a small upright stone which may well have been another in the group of three remaining stones.[64]

The nearness of the lesser standing stone to the Burry Menhir suggests that it may have been associated with it in some way. It stands 1.6m high, just over half the original height of the Burry Menhir. The top is furrowed and uneven, and it has been suggested that the unevenness of the top may have resulted in the upper part breaking off, but it is impossible to say whether the break occurred before or after its erection.[65] It is thought that the pair once formed an east-west arc on the skyline and may have been used to indicate the equinox, when day and night are of equal length. A small V-shaped cut in the horizon on Rhossili Down may also have been used to serve the same purpose.

The Burry Standing Stone, stands about 2.2m high and is 0.6m thick. This is not the tallest in Gower (that honour goes to Carreg Bica), but it is the most impressive because it has not been incorporated into a field boundary. It is roughly pillar-shaped and triangular at its base, but it is not known whether the unusual shape had any significance for those who erected it.

Carreg Bica

Standing Stone
Location: On Mynydd Drumau, about 2km north-west of Neath
(SS 724 994)
Access: Public footpaths from the north, south and east

The stone can be approached by public paths from three directions. This explanation is of the route from the south. From the A465 Vale of Neath road and turn north onto the A474 to Pontardawe. At the first roundabout, just north of the A465, turn left towards Neath Abbey. Keep on this road for about half a mile until, just beyond a zebra crossing, you turn right just before reaching Cwrt Lwydi Gwyn care home. This road soon passes under a high viaduct and curls up the hill. Park just beyond the end of the 30mph speed zone, and walk up the footpath which starts on tarmac by the entrance to The Coach House. Keep to the main path, which zig-zags up the hill through woodland, eventually depositing you near the crest of the hill by a ruined building. Keep to the well marked path which shadows the rim of the hill until you reach older woodland, where another path crosses at right angles alongside a stone wall. Follow the path and stone wall to Carreg Bica.

Carreg Bica is an isolated standing stone formed of local sandstone which stands about 4.3m in height. It is incorporated into a later field wall. Despite being the largest in the area its purpose, like so many others in Glamorganshire, is obscure. It could mark a burial, an ancient trackway, or have had some long forgotten ritual significance. To the north of the stone are two large stone gate posts, which are thought may have formed a single standing stone at one time.[66]

Carreg Bica means 'the pointed stone'. Its other name is Maen Bradwen or 'the stone of Bradwen'. Bradwen was probably a local mythological hero, one of the many giants, elves and goblins believed to have populated Neath in far off days. There is a local tradition that on Good Friday the children of Skewen would race from the village to the stone. This custom survived until the 1930s.[67] There is also a legend that states that the stone visits the river Nedd for a drink whenever it hears the cock crow.[68]

Carn Llechart Cairn Circle

> Ring Cairn
> Location: Pontardawe (SS 697 063)
> Access: On open hillside crossed by private paths

Take the A474 Pontardawe to Gwaun Cae Gurwen Road. At Rhyd y fro village take the minor road west opposite The Traveller's Well and by A&M Transport Services. About 1km along you reach Coed Cae Mawr farmhouse and you want to park in one of the small lay-bys/passing places along this road. Walk up the track that heads off onto the hill a few hundred yards along the road from Coed Cae Mawr. The cairn circle is found after about 0.5km near the top of the middle height of the hill, back towards Rhyd-y-fro.

Carn Llechart is one of the largest cairn circles to be found in the country. It also has the distinction of being mentioned in one of the earliest antiquarian books, William Camden's *Britannia* (1695 edition), and dates to the first half of the second millennium BC. It is made up of 25 upright thin slabs, most leaning outwards, arranged in a rough circle 14m across which encloses a central burial cist with the capstone missing. There is no evidence of a covering mound.

Alongside the ancient trackway 400m north-west of Carn Llechart are the remains of about 16 stony mounds of varying size, which appear to be a Bronze Age cemetery. Several more, insignificant, cairns are found dotted along the ridge which was also used as a burial ground long before Carn Llechart was built. A short distance

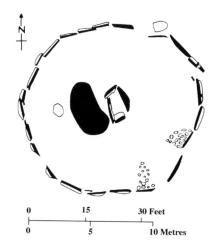

N

0	15	30 Feet

0	5	10 Metres

to the south-west is a ruined Neolithic Tomb of which only three of the slabs remain upright and which used to form a small burial chamber set up against a natural outcrop, with a displaced capstone on the east side. The poor state of this tomb may possibly be due to the Bronze Age builders robbing materials for their cairns.

Interestingly, in the field south of the circle is a new stone circle. In the winter of 1989, a local farmer decided, for reasons best known to himself, to rearrange the boulders in his field, which will no doubt confuse generations of archaeologists in years to come!

Whilst in the vicinity, it is worth making a slight detour to Cefn Gwrhyd which, like many ridgeways, was used as a natural trackway by ancient travellers. The remaining monuments and funerary relics lie scattered about in bleak places. A minor road snakes along the ridge, staring from the A474 at Rhyd y fro and passing Llangiwg Church. The road then climbs onto the open moorland and after 900m there is a gorse and heather covered mound on the left hand side. This is known as Carn Llwyd, now unimpressive, but according to antiquarian accounts it was once very similar to Carn Llechart with three concentric rings of upright stones surrounding a central cist. When William Morgan reported on it in the last century, only a few stones remained and all have now disappeared. Along the ridge five more cairns can be seen, but are some distance from the road and are not easy to locate even with an OS map. In the same area, a much more obvious monument is a fallen standing stone which is on the right hand side, where the road begins its decent to Gwrhyd Chapel. The stone has now been incorporated into a dry-stone wall on the edge of a field, and when it was first erected it would have stood at least 4m high, making it one of the tallest standing stones in Glamorganshire.

Graig Fawr Ring Cairn

Ring Cairn
Location: South of Pontardulais (SS 628 066)
Access: By public footpath

Take the minor road from Ammanford to Llangyfelach. At the small hamlet of Gerdinen take the footpath west onto the ridge. The site is 1km to the west, just west of the north-south trackway.

Overlooking the Loughor Valley is the broad moorland of Graig Fawr, where it appears that this ring cairn has lain undisturbed for 3,500 years. The arrangement is unusual in that it has a small circle within and against the edge of a larger one. Sites such as this could have had both ritual and sepulchral functions. Interestingly, the outer ring is an almost perfect circle and is formed by two stony banks separated by a shallow depression from which the stones for the banks were presumably dug. The main entrance appears to be a gap on the north-east side, with a lesser one on the south side. The smaller inner circle, formed by a low bank and shallow external ditch, has no apparent entrance. This site has not been excavated, but sites with a similar arrangement that have been excavated have been found to contain a cremation burial in the inner circle, and palisades around both circles. The absence of any entrance through the inner circle makes it highly unlikely that this was a hut enclosure.

The Graig Fawr ridge is rich in Bronze Age burials monuments, and it is thought that during the Bronze Age it was principally used as a vast cemetery. The remains of more than 40 cairns are scattered across the moor and most of the mounds can be located easily, although others only appear as innocuous stony patches.

Penlle'rbebyll

Ring Cairn
Location: In the mountains between Pontardulais
and Pontardawe (SN 635 048)
Access: By roadside

Take the minor road from Llangyfelach towards Garnswllt. 2km
north of Felindre, the cairn is just to the east of the road near the
summit.

Penlle'rbebyll, which means the 'high place of the encampment', is an unusual ring cairn near to the summit of Mynydd
Pysgodlyn, the mountains between Pontardulais and Pontardawe. It
comprises a horseshoe-shaped earth bank with a shallow external
ditch which would appear, originally, to have completely encircled
the bank. There is a wide entrance gap on the south side which is
partly blocked by a smaller enclosure. Mr. William Morgan
suggests that it was used as a medieval encampment built to contain
victims of the plague.[69] Although it does resemble a small dwelling
hut with an adjoining yard or cattle pound, archaeologic evidence
proves that the outer ring is of a well-established Bronze Age type,
whilst its remote and inhospitable setting suggest a Bronze Age
origin. However, the inner enclosure is less easy to define. The
whole monument is now turf-covered.

This, like other sites at Cefn Bryn and Graig Fawr may have
been an elaborate ritual enclosure.

Pen y Crug

Burial Mound
Location: South-east of Llanrhidian (SS 511 914)
Access: On open ground criss-crossed by paths

Take the B4271 road towards Swansea from Llanrhidian. About 2km along take the right turn towards Reynoldstown. Park near the Broad Pool which lies about half a kilometre down this road on the right. Pen y Crug lies towards the field boundaries to the north of the pool, between lines of telegraph poles.

The mound, some 24m across and 1.2m high is best viewed in early spring or autumn as it becomes densely covered with summer bracken. There is evidence of a central pit, but this may have been dug by early excavators carrying out work that has been unrecorded.[70]

The Iron Age

An Overview of the Celtic People

Our knowledge of the Neolithic and Bronze Age periods in Wales is, to a great extent, founded on the study of burial sites and the discovery of stone and bronze implements. However, in studying the Iron Age or Celtic period, 600 BC - AD 48, burials from this period are almost unknown in Britain and information obtained from the few sites is meagre to say the least. In addition, very few iron objects from this period have survived centuries of decomposition. Nevertheless, not all is lost. Thanks to the practise of the Iron Age people, or Celts as they have become known world-wide, in building defensive hillforts they have provided sufficient evidence to enable archaeologists to piece together a reasonable picture of the Age. Inside these forts posthole evidence has helped to form images of their houses and granaries, whilst the artefacts that have survived demonstrate a more structured and domesticated way of life than that which preceded. For the first time, the archaeological evidence shifts from burials to settlements. Towards the end of the period, there also start to be a number of written reports by classical writers.

The oldest archaeological traces of the Celtic races can be found in the Austrian Alps in Hallstatt, a large salt-mining area near Salzburg. Here is the earliest evidence of iron-workings, the word 'iron' in fact being derived from the Celtic word *isarnos*. These people traded salt throughout Europe, and the Museum at Hallstatt contains well preserved items of this activity—gloves for sliding down the wooden struts of the mineshaft, a hod made of timber and leather used to transport the salt to the collection point within the mountain, together with a leather hat and fragments of clothing.

Today we take salt very much for granted, but then it was much sought after, not only as a flavourer, but also as an excellent preservative for meat stored for use in the winter months and as essential for life. Evidence of salt mining has also been discovered in Britain, but not, as yet, in Glamorganshire.

Although it is possible that tribes of Celtic origin existed in Britain and Ireland as early as 2000 BC, it has traditionally been accepted that the Iron Age began in Britain around 600 BC when Celtic ideas were either disseminated along the trade routes, or through immigration, or possibly invasion or some combination of these. There were several well-established trading routes to Britain. One was the main tin-trading route from Asia Minor, known as the Phoenician Trading Route, to Cornwall which was then the largest tin producing area in the Western world. A second route led from south-west Germany and Switzerland where the tribes had other trading links with the Eastern Mediterranean. A third route lay along the coast of the Iberian Peninsula to south Wales, whilst another lay through Gaul, with trade routes from southern Germany and eastern France.

Amongst scholars there exist two main opinions regarding the Iron Age people. Some identify them with the dark-haired, broad-headed Armenoids (Alpine race), whilst others prefer to associate them with the fair long-headed people of northern Europe. It is, of course, possible that they were not a pure race, but rather a mix of peoples who were influenced at different periods and by different cultures which developed into what we know today as the Celtic culture. What is certain is that they were fearless warriors who liked bright colours and glittering ornaments. They were also skilled craftsmen who, later in the Iron Age, were squeezed out of southern Europe and Gaul by the Romans and were eager to seek new lands in which to settle and establish their culture.

On reaching Britain the early Celts formed military aristocracies and dominated large areas. They built hilltop settlements known today as hillforts which were protected by single or multiple banks and ditches, some very complex in nature. Those who settled in the west, called the Goidel Celts, brought with them a language which is the forerunner of modern day Welsh. They forced many of the native families to cross over to Ireland, the Isle of Man or northwards and where they formed the Gaelic race. The remainder of the Bronze Age peoples settled into a peaceful co-existence with the new arrivals.

However, the date of their arrival, like so many other theories, must now be questioned. Radiocarbon dating and continual re-assessment of some of the archaeological finds show that many of the 'Iron Age' hillforts were built in the late Bronze Age. We do know that this was a period of great unrest in Northern and Central Europe, but there is nothing to suggest a mass influx of people. The most likely explanation is that there was a gradual influx of people into Britain over a long period of time, and like all periods in history the two cultures would have run parallel, each taking and adapting ideas from the other.

For convenience the Iron Age has been divided into three periods, Early or Hallstatt (600-400 BC), La Tene (400-200 BC) and later or Belgic (200 BC to the Roman conquest), but it is highly likely that the Iron Age had begun to take a hold around 1000 BC.

The Iron Ages

The early Iron Age is often referred to as the period of transition, a time when the early settlers absorbed or subdued the Bronze Age peoples. Unfortunately, to date, no early Iron Age structures nor a sufficient number of artefacts of the period have been found to clearly show the transitional process in Glamorganshire. All that is known for certain is that by the time of the Roman conquest, Glamorganshire had a Celtic society.

Nevertheless, one famous find, discovered in 1911, may cast some light on the hazy period between the Bronze and Iron Ages as many of the objects are typical of the late Bronze Age. In 1910 work began on the drainage of a small natural mountain lake at Llyn Fawr, south of Hirwaun (SS 917 035), so that it could be adapted as a reservoir. In this extremely isolated spot, overshadowed by a steep precipice and surrounded by a circle of rocky slopes, 24 remarkable objects relating to a ritual were discovered.[71] Even more intriguing is how they came to be there. To arrive at the site these early settlers would have found it necessary to take an arduous journey across the high, windswept plateau with its deep trough-like valleys. Whether these were new arrivals to the country who landed at Swansea Bay and made they way to the Rhigos Mountains, or a second generation of immigrants who had made their way along the south Wales coast to the Severn Estuary is unknown.

Within the find, which is now on display at the National Museum of Wales in Cardiff, were two fine beaten bronze and iron cauldrons, a series of six socketed bronze axes, three bronze chisels or gouges, an assortment of bronze sickles, and a bronze razor. Interestingly, the razor is not an ordinary two edged Bronze Age type, but a single edged example similar to that found amongst the Hallstatt Celts who had settled in Burgundy. Even more intriguing are a series of iron items including a spearhead, a sickle and part of a sword. The Bronze Age type sickle is unique because it is an exact copy, in iron, of a native bronze one and is the most striking example known to show the adaptation from bronze to iron. It can safely be assumed that this was the work of a craftsman trained in Bronze Age traditions, but who had now learnt to work skilfully with a new material which had not yet been established as a traditional metal. The sword fragment is interesting as it is also of the Hallstatt type, with bone riveted plates. This is the only one of its type to be found in Britain and is obviously an import.[72] The origin of the spearhead is unknown—it may be local or belonging to the Hallstatt Burgundy race.

The Bronze objects also included two bronze pony cheek pieces, three bronze discs from a harness decoration, an open work harness mount and a belt hook. These are very similar to those found at Court St. Etienne in Belgium and in a Celtic cemetery in Hallstatt. In *Celtic World*, Barry Cunliffe states that the domesticated horse had been introduced into Europe before the arrival of the Celts, and suggests that the horse may have been harnessed as far back as the Upper Palaeolithic.

By the late Bronze Age, the horse was harnessed in yokes with bridles of leather, and, possibly, mouth pieces of leather. By the beginning of the Hallstatt period Bronze horse gear was common throughout Europe, as the horse became more widely used from around 700BC. As much of the horse harness and equipment of this period, including that found in Llyn Fawr, bears a strong resemblance to that used by the horse-riding communities occupying the Pontie steppes, it may be that the people who settled on this mountain in Wales belonged to a group known as the Thraco-Cimmerian. These were wild horsemen who swept west from the steppes and if not actually settling in Wales, were probably responsible for the spread of knowledge of horse-riding and the associated equipment, as well as iron technology in which they were proficient.

Evidence that metal working was carried out at Merthyr Mawr has been proven by the presence of iron-slag, bronze droplets and fragments of small crucibles. There are also a few examples, such as the fine ring-head pin recovered from Minchin Hole, of early metal working on the Gower Peninsula. Equally as interesting as the evidence of metal working, is a set of at least eight delicately carved bone spoons. This immediately conjures up an image of an early Celtic family sharing a meal together or maybe they were the very first love spoons that we associate with the Welsh of today? A more likely explanation though, and not so romantic, is that they were tradesman's wares destined for exchange or bartering.

The Middle Iron Age period is seen as the period when a second influx of people, or their ideas, established the more characteristic Celtic culture, equivalent to the continental La Tene Iron Age. La Tene was an Iron Age settlement on Lake Lleuchatel in Switzerland from where a large deposit of metal ware has been recovered. The remains of a bridge, and possibly a jetty, were revealed at the eastern end of the lake. In the deep mud beside these timbers archaeologists from Zurich found a profusion of finely developed metalwork including examples of the elaborately enamelled horse and chariot decorations that are associated with the Celtic culture, as well as remnants of their distinctive, brightly coloured clothing. Many fine examples from this period, which help to build up a picture of these Celtic tribes, can today be seen in British and European Museums. These people may have crossed from France to the east and south coasts and spread west and north. Besides introducing the fine decorative art style, they also introduced the two wheeled war chariot drawn by specially bred small ponies, similar to the modern Welsh pony.

The only important examples of La Tene decorative ware to be found in West Glamorganshire have been found at Nant-y Cafn, near Seven Sisters in the Dulais Valley. This extensive collection of objects consisted of ornamental horse-trappings and tankard handles. Some of the objects were decorated with white and red enamel, whilst others included items made of brass, an alloy of copper and zinc, which was introduced into Britain by the Romans.

This find, deposited around AD 50-75 may have belonged to the Roman occupation, but are included here because they are representative of the La Tene style.[73] It has been suggested that, as the hoard contained objects of Roman and military equipment, it had been deposited by a native craftsman who may have obtained the materials or goods by trading with the Romans, and feared reprisals from his neighbours. Also included with this hoard was a bronze chisel, two small bells, and a bronze weight which was of a similar standard to one found at Mainz.[74]

Another interesting, but ill recorded discovery was made in 1818 at Castell y Lligaid during excavation for limestone on the east side of Ogmore Down. This site has been identified as a rare Iron Age cemetery. Unfortunately, the finds were lost shortly afterwards, though a summary description and a few rough sketches drawn at the time have survived.[75] The field name Castell y Lligaid has also been lost, but it is considered to have been about ST 905 753. Just two feet below ground labourers uncovered at least three inhumation burials (it seems the Iron Age Celts abandoned cremation and reverted to inhumation). The skulls were capped with bronze helmets which a sketch shows to have been of the conical type adopted by Celts from Italy as early as the fifth century BC. Two of the helmets had silver finials on the top, each weighing an ounce, from which, on each side, two twisted gold and silver wires were carried down to hold up two hinged cheek guards when they were not in use. These guards were made from gold alloy and decorated with red enamel. On Italian-Celtic helmets they were a prominent feature but, if the sketches are accurate, those found were small and therefore only for ornamental purposes. In addition there were two copper skull caps, each nearly a quarter of an inch thick, and one or two pieces of a brass chain that were found nearby. It was not recorded whether the skull-caps were worn under the helmets, although it seems probable. The helmet, however, was rarely used by the Celts and so this may have been a find from a high status burial. With insufficient evidence, mystery will continue to surround these finds.

The concentration of metal goods found around the Merthyr Mawr area and the Ogmore estuary has led to the suggestion by Savory that the people of western Brittany may have played a role in spreading metalwork throughout south Wales.[76] Savory backed his theory by citing a pot from Bacon Hole, a mould discovered at Worm's Head, and two La Tene bracelets found at Coygan Camp, on the opposite side of the Burry Estuary.[77]

During the later Iron Age period a new influx of people settled in Wales due to the pressures on the minor kingdoms of Gaul and southern Britain from the Romans. These were the Belgic peoples, possibly the most progressive of the Celts, who introduced the art of enamelling to these shores, as well as the god and cult symbols that were so cherished in Gaul. They were also the only people of Celtic origin for whom we have direct documentary evidence of their migration to Britain. A new type of pottery also came into use, similar to that found in areas known to have been occupied by the Belgic peoples.

In summary these three different Iron Age periods can be clearly seen throughout the excavations of the various settlements and by examination of the finds.

Hillforts and Settlements

It appears that, whereas the Neolithic and Bronze Age people spent a great deal of their time and energy building tombs for the dead, the Iron Age people preferred to concentrate their building efforts on communities and comforts for the living. Armed with basic equipment such as antler picks, oxen shoulder blades and wicker baskets they set about changing the landscape by constructing massive, defended settlements. What remains today is an abundance of splendid hillforts—almost 600 in Wales alone, approximately one fifth of the British total—which were built to protect them from unwanted intruders, and were built on such a scale that many have lasted for 2,500 years.

As well as the hillforts, three other types of dwelling have been defined in the Glamorganshire area. Several caves known to the Neolithic and Bronze Age settlers were also occupied during the Iron Age, though it is not certain if these were only used in unsettled times of trouble, or were permanent dwellings. Only a few coastal relics of Iron Age date have been discovered in Glamorganshire, the most prominent of these at Bacon Hole and Culver Hole in Gower. Iron Age pottery has been found in both these caves although not in sufficient quantity to indicate permanent settlement.

Most of the nine headlands on the south and west coast of Gower are known to have been defended and occupied during the Iron Age and well into the Roman period. These coastal hillforts, known as promontory forts, are all small with the emphasis apparently on individually defended settlements, each large enough to house the owner, his family and a considerable entourage. A possible explanation for the low number of dwellings within the sites could be that these forts were used primarily as places of refuge; perhaps the only building large enough to leave surface traces belonged to permanent inhabitants, with the rest of the site only accommodating people in times of trouble. Again, the banks of the 'fort' might have been used like fences in which to corral stock. The absence of large hillforts in the south and west of Glamorganshire suggests that there was no centralised government in the area but rather many small family units. The remains of a further promontory fort of interest can be found at Merthyr Mawr Warren, near Porthcawl.[78]

Just outside the area covered by this book are two large hut settlements that were not enclosed, one at Carreg Lwyd overlooking the head of Rhondda Fawr (SN 922 018), and the other at Buarth Maen (SO 012 053), located on a shelf sloping towards the south. Both these sites are unusual as the settlements are very high up and in an exposed position. It is possible that they may have had a special pastoral function and were occupied only during the summer months. Excavations during 1921 at Carreg Lwyd found evidence of leather, iron and iron slag.[79] The Buarth Maen site remains more or less undisturbed and comprises three main enclosures, not all complete, and some short lengths of walling as well as some round huts. Unfortunately the few finds at these sites are insufficient to enable archaeologists to establish whether they date from the Iron Age or the Roman period, or both. A fine example of a reconstructed village community can been seen at Castell Henllys, near Newport in Pembrokeshire. Here the visitor can walk around wattle and daub round huts, animal shelters and storerooms, and learn more about a typical Celtic settlement.

Excavations in other parts of Wales have revealed that the hillforts in the Glamorganshire area varied considerably in design and size, but it can be assumed that each must represent the home of a

'Iron Age' housing at Castell Henllys, Pembrokeshire

thriving community. Some settlements consisted of a series of round huts grouped together within an enclosure whilst others contained streets of houses set out in much the same way as in present day towns. The finest example in Wales is at Tre'r Caer in the north. This well preserved, five acre site is enclosed within a rampart, and inside are the remains of some 50 huts of varying shapes and sizes, as well as from different periods. Where total excavation has taken place on smaller sites it has been noted that a simple arrangement of circular huts were placed in the centre of the site, with storage buildings around the periphery. It has also been shown that individual structures had been replaced on a number of occasions, whilst all the enclosures were sited not far from a permanent supply of water.

The Iron Age people of the middle period were the great fort builders, and it is their handiwork that we see today. These strongholds must have been built by vast communal effort and would have taken many man-hours to construct. They were built on prominent sites chosen for their far-reaching views, so that any threat of attack could be seen well in advance. Excavation has revealed that many of these sites went through a process of progressive construction which

'Iron Age' housing at Castell Henllys, Pembrokeshire

elaborated on the original plan, providing a series of massive earthen ramparts to enclose both inhabitants and livestock. They were predominately farming settlements with circular huts.

Over the years gateways were improved from basic simple gaps by curving the rampart ends inwards and building stronger, bastion-like gateways. Defence was further improved by turning an original single rampart fort into a double rampart or even a multi-rampart one. This would have put the settlement in greater safety by increasing its distance from attackers using slings.

The finest of these hillforts are in the south and west of Britain, such as Dissbury, St. Catherine's Hill and Maiden Castle in Dorset, where the central plateau alone measures 35 acres and beyond which is a series of four banks and ditches, with complicated systems of gateway entrances increasing the area yet further.

However, much of the variety in hillforts is due to the choice of site and local building material available. A study of those within the area of this book show that the most common example is the contour fort, where the main rampart follows a natural brow on the landscape and used any available crags or cliffs to make the building task easier. Another style, known as a concentric hillfort is usually found on a hill slope rather than a hilltop. These have widely spaced concentric banks and entrances which often face downhill and therefore suggest that defence was not necessarily a priority in their siting. Those who had decided to settle near the coast built promontory forts which necessitated constructing defences across only a narrow neck of ground. Most of this type cover less than one hectare (2.47 acres). These settlements most likely served as simple shelters rather than as permanently manned forts although some of the smallest would have been fortified homesteads for people who farmed the surrounding land, or used them as a focal point for tribal power.

By far the largest Iron Age settlements on the Gower Peninsula are the Bulwark Hillfort (SS 443 928) on Llanmadoc Hill, the cluster of three forts that straddle Hardings Down on the west end of the Gower Peninsula (SS 434 908, 437 906 and 437 908), and the Cil Ifor Top Hillfort near Llanridian (SS 505 923). These are also some of the most outstanding examples of the concentric hillforts in the county.

Domestic Life

Artefacts from Iron Age sites in Glamorganshire and throughout Britain have enabled a picture of domestic life to be formed. An abundance of fragmented pottery has been found consisting of a wide range of ceramics such as storage vessels, large and small jugs, bowls and plates, each with its unique function. Analysis of the clay used in their manufacture indicates that most were made locally and not bought through trading with others. Pottery similar to Glastonbury style wares and dating from the first century BC has been found at the Knave, a promontory fort near Rhossili (SS 432884). Occupation of the site, however, may have begun much earlier. The quarter acre fort at Bishopston Valley has produced pottery of a similar date and Samian ware which suggests a continued occupation well into the Roman period. The pottery found at the High Pennard fort, a two acre site with widely spaced ramparts included only Roman objects.

The plough, so vital in the Neolithic period continued to be of value during the Iron Age. Ploughs found in peat bogs throughout north-west Europe indicate that two types were being used—the light plough or ard, and the heavy plough. The ard scratched a furrow in the soil, whilst the heavy plough could turn a furrow. It was the ard that was in common use in Britain during the Celtic period, and it appears that it was necessary to plough each field twice in order to break up the soil, the second ploughing being at right angles to the first. From other evidence it can be deduced that at harvest time the ears of corn were cut with iron sickles and brought to the village for cleaning and threshing. The husks were used for animal fodder and the grain placed in stores with raised floors to allow the air to circulate; it is probable that the whole community would have been involved in the harvest. Later, the animals were brought in from the upland pastures to forage the stubble in the field. This helped to break up the earth and the animals' manure helped to replenish the fertility in time for the sowing season.

Finds of cauldron hangers and fire-dogs confirm the importance of the hearth in the domestic home. The classical writers are all in agreement about Celtic feasts, which were noisy, drunken and with much exaggerated boasting. Diodorus Siculus wrote in *Bibliotheca Historica*, 'They also invite strangers to their banquets, and only after the meal do they ask who they are and what they stand in need. At dinner they are wont to be moved by chance remarks to wordy disputes, and to fight in single combat, regarding their lives as naught.'

Drink was important and a communal cup was carried from person to person by a slave. As Posidonius recorded in his *Histories*, 'The slave serves the cup towards the right not the left, then they drink a little at a time, not more than a mouthful, but they do it rather often.' Various foods would have been served and Strabo, in his *Geographica*, says 'They have large quantities of food together with all kinds of meat especially fresh and salt pork.' The evidence of the importance of pork is confirmed in graves, as many dead men had been provided with a joint of pork or even a whole pig for his first feast in the afterworld.

The feast was also a time when the clan would reminisce about past exploits and heroes. There is little doubt that at times such as these a bard would sing or recite traditional tribal songs and sagas. Again, Siculus tells us that there were 'lyric poets' who would sing to the accompaniment of instruments resembling lyres.

A large number of pins have been found, which were later replaced by brooches as clothing fasteners. These were used to fasten cloaks at the chest or at the shoulder, and they were often worn in pairs joined by a chain. From both archaeological evidence across Europe and the classical writers we learn that the Celts wore trousers, tunics and cloaks, all brightly coloured. It is possible that the tartans of the Scottish clans of today are a direct descendent of the Celtic tradition.

Archaeological finds have also included loom weights, spindle-whorls and querns, bone needles and weaving combs all of which point to a domesticated way of life.

Celts as Warriors

Much has been written about the war-like nature of the Celts. There are reports that the early Celts were a volatile, militaristic race that had much to contend with because of the constant pressure exerted on them from the north and east by the Germanic tribes and, from the south, by the ever-expanding Roman Empire. They settled in northern Italy after invading Rome in 390 BC before their nomadic and warfaring nature took them on as far as Greece, where records show that they invaded Delphi in 297 BC.

However, during the second century BC Roman military strength increased. The Romans conquered southern and central France before moving northwards to conquer Gallia Belgica in the middle of the first century BC. As a consequence the Celts were forced further northwards and it was at this time that most arrived in Britain.

The impression of the Celts as war-makers is further substantiated by the abundance of fine Iron Age artistic and military artefacts that have been uncovered. The literary evidence also states that they were a warrior élite who displayed a prowess that was a prominent feature of their life, a world of thundering chariots and splendid weapons. But could this have been the equipment of an invading race, or ornate gifts brought along to exchange between tribal chieftains? The chariot was not new in Europe, in fact examples have been found in Sweden depicted on tombs of the tenth century BC. But it was not until the third and second centuries BC, in the hands of the Celts, that the chariot came into its own.

Warfare cannot be discussed without mentioning the Celtic mythology of head hunting, considered to be the centre of all strength and wisdom. The Iron Age Celt, unlike their Celtic Christian descendants, gloried in battle. Defeated warriors from another tribe were decapitated and the heads taken back to the settlement, embalmed in cedar oil and hung on posts outside the victor's hut for all to see and admire. They believed that the strength contained in these heads would assist them in future battles and many such skulls have been discovered 'guarding' sacred wells, temples and shrines. Livy, the Roman historian, further informs us that the heads were cleaned out, gilded and then filled with holy water and used as a sacred vessel for ritual drinking.[80] The cult of the severed head was also reflected in later Welsh literature. In the *Mabinogion* the head of the god Bran directs events long after it has been severed from its body.

Horsemanship

The Celts were expert in horsemanship and use of the chariot. They decorated their horses and chariots with ornaments, decked themselves in fine gold-chased buckles, torcs and bracelets, which would have been an impressive sight when they glistened in the sunlight. It has been reported that these fearless warriors, woad-smeared and often naked, except for a gold torc worn to give them strength, sped into battle in their war chariots, hurling javelins at their enemy before dismounting and attacking them with swords. Horses became a symbol of the aristocratic warrior élite, and the horseman and the charioteer were people of high status within Celtic Society. In addition the horse was also revered because of its qualities of beauty, speed, sexual vigour and fertility.

In Celtic mythology the horse was worshiped by Epona, the horse goddess, who appears on nearly 300 stone monuments in Gaul. Her name derives from the Celtic word for horse and she usually appears side-saddle astride or between two horses or foals, one male, one female.

Celtic Beliefs and Mythologies

The beliefs of the pagan Celt have been pieced together using classical manuscripts and archaeological sources, and although very little solid evidence of their beliefs has been found in Glamorganshire we can assume that those who lived in the area would have followed common ideals.

Celtic belief and worship was based around the natural and animate world. Great significance was placed on trees because they were known to survive longer than man and therefore some mystique and sacredness was attached to them. The Godelic alphabet, the ogham script which was used by the druids, the elders of the Celtic tribes, was based on seasonal trees. The alphabet was combined with 13 'timespans', which formed the basis of a yearly calendar. Each timespan was linked to its seasonal tree. To discuss the customs and beliefs surrounding all 13 trees is beyond the scope of this book, but it is worth mentioning two, the oak and the yew, which are still regarded with reverence by many to this day.

Unlike the Bronze Age people, the Celts did not worship in stone sun temples, but in oak groves, which they honoured as holy places. As Pliny the Elder recorded in his *Natural History*, 'Nothing is more sacred to the druids than the mistletoe and the tree on which it grows, especially if it be an oak. They chose oak woods for their sacred groves, and performed sacred rites without using oak branches. Whatever grows on the tree is sent from heaven, a sign that the tree has been chosen by god.'

The wood from the oak was important too. At the source of the River Seine 140 wooden figures were found—all made from oak. Near Scarborough, a burial was discovered in an oak coffin, with oak branches and mistletoe carefully laid inside. It is even thought that the word 'druid' means 'wise man of the oak', and an old Welsh word, *dergen* is thought to mean 'son of the oak'.

After some pioneering work by Allen Meredith, a housemaster at a Hertfordshire school, it has been proved that the yew is far older than originally believed. It is probably one of the oldest species of tree in the world, and could even pre-date the giant redwood and bristlecome pine of America, which are currently accepted as the world's oldest species.[81]

The yew has a strong association with Christianity as it is found in many of Britain's churchyards. In fact, most of the 400 largest yew trees in Britain are situated on church ground, and it has been thought that is was so because the evergreen foliage was seen as a symbol of everlasting life. Allen Meredith's theory is part of an argument that turns everything around, and it could be that churches were built around the yew because the early beliefs of the Celts and their predecessors were integrated into Christian practice. It is also thought that the druids inscribed their sacred words in ogham script on wood cut from yews.

The ancient Celts were also extremely interested in natural wells, springs, pools and sources of rivers. Most probably they believed these to be entrances to the underworld, another important feature in their mythology. With no great burial monuments to the Iron Age dead it is generally believed that, as water was so important to the Celtic culture, rivers, lakes and other wet areas were used as the final resting-place for the dead.

The Celts also believed in 'shift-shaping', and claimed that the gods were able to appear in animal form as and when they chose. As such therefore, certain animals were also considered to be sacred and regarded as totems, a tribal badge or emblem.

Perhaps the most important symbol for the Celts was the wild boar. It represented war and hunting, hospitality and feasting. As a war symbol it represented ferocity and the Celts believed that its spirit would make their warriors fearless in battle. Boar headed trumpets were used in warfare and boar figurines were used on helmets and crests.

Lord over all the animals was Cernunnos, the horned god who was seen by the Celts as the ruler of the natural world. The earliest known example of Cernunnos appears on a fourth century BC rock carving in the Camorica Valley in northern Italy. He usually appears sitting crossed-legged with two twisted torcs and antlers and accompanied by a stag, ram-horned snake and other creatures. British evidence for Cernunnos is rare. However, a recent find at Petersfield in Hampshire of a Celtic silver coin dating from around AD 20 includes an image of the god.

Celtic Currency
As most of the early Celtic tribes were nomadic, their main possessions served as portable currency. It was only when they came into contact with the Greek and Roman civilisations, whose coinage systems were already well established, that they began to adapt to

the world of coinage instead of bartering. Polybus, a leading citizen of Megalopolis, wrote of the Celts in his *Histories*,[82] 'They live in unwalled villages, without superfluous furniture, for as they slept on beds of leaves, and fed on meat, and were extensively occupied with war and agriculture, their lives were very simple ... Their possessions consisted of cattle and gold, because these were the only things they could carry about with them everywhere according to the circumstances, and shift where they chose.'

The first coinage minted in Britain was used during the La Tene period and was copied from Macedonian silver coins. Virtually all Greek coins were of silver, whereas those minted by the first Celts were of gold—no doubt reflecting the Celts love of bright objects. It is possibly that the very first coins were small gold rings, some-times described as 'ring' money.[83] The gold 'stater' was one of the most highly prized Celtic coins, and it is said that on one occasion soldiers were paid one gold stater each for an entire campaign!

At a later date, lower denomination Celtic coins were introduced in silver, and these were used for everyday transactions. A third and even lower denomination coin was also available in the form of 'potin' money. These coins were minted in strips, which were then cut into weighed units. Potin coins were made from a tin alloy, with much of the tin used coming from the Cornish tin mines.

Celtic coinage continues to prove elusive with very few finds, and almost none in Glamorganshire. Those discovered elsewhere were undated, in our sense of the term, with little or no inscription so it is difficult for the archaeologist to assess their distribution or even to identify them.

Conclusion

So what do the finds and evidence on the landscape tell us about the Celtic people? It shows that the Celts were a capable and clever race who brought a precise social order to Wales, one which grad-ually evolved into an ordered tribal system. They did what the 'men of stone' and the 'men of bronze' could not do. They became the masters of the heavy clay soil, and battled with the wild and rugged land. It appears that agriculture was the way of life for the common Iron Age peoples. They ploughed the fields and hewed down the trees, but within their hillforts they established a ruling class with the main focus on loyalty to the clan rather than the tribe. In fact the word Celt itself is derived from the Gaelic word *clann* meaning a kindred sprit.

The noble clansmen believed they shared a common ancestor, even though that ancestor may have been mythical rather than human. Below them were the farmers who tilled the land and raised the livestock. Then came the craftsmen who made everyday life easier for the people, and fashioned the ornate goods prized by their superiors. The third group were the serfs or the servants who worked as slaves for, and therefore were dependent upon the clan for their survival and well being. This lowest group may have consisted of the captives they chose not to kill, or people who had arrived from outside the clan system for some other reason.

The success of each hillfort was largely governed by the land that supplied their needs. The rearing of cattle played an important part in the economy because these animals served as a symbol of wealth which could be converted into extra currency when the need arose. In the more mountainous regions sheep may have been more prevalent, but positive proof is not available. For the Celts wealth was measured by the droves of cattle, horses, swine and sheep they owned. Life centred around the seasonal calendar with everyone helping with cereal production.

There is much evidence for prehistoric fields and field systems in Britain, remains often surviving on hill slopes. They are marked by a low bank or lynchets at the bottom of the lower slope formed through soil creep. The fields tend to be square in shape to facilitate cross ploughing and are often roughly the size of a squared-up football pitch, varying from 0.16 to 0.25 hectares. Very few sites have been excavated, but Butser Ancient Farm in Hampshire grows prehistoric varieties of wheat, some dating back to 7000BC.

It is believed that it was the Romans who gave the hillfort dwellers of south Wales the name of Silures. The Roman chroniclers informed us that the Silures were not typical of the fair skinned people we associate as northern Europeans, but were dark-skinned and curly-headed. Scapula noted their '*Praecipua Silurum pervicacia*'—extraordinary stubbornness, and it was a stubbornness that took the Romans 25 years to break.

Three forts, Hardings Down

Hillforts
Location: Hardings Down, to the south of Llangenydd
(SS 434 908, SS 437 906, SS 437 908)
Access: Various public footpaths lead onto Hardings Down

On the edge of Llangenydd village take the track to the south onto Hardings Down. There are various well signposted footpaths. The three forts are on the top and to the north of the hill, quite close together. They are all different, and may well have served different purposes. Whether they are contemporary with each other remains a question for further investigation.

The most complete is the westernmost one (SS 434 908), which has a substantial single bank and defence ditch. The main enclosure measuring 110m by 75m is roughly oval in shape. Excavations were carried out by the Royal Commission on Ancient and Historical Monuments in 1962 to determine whether it had similar structures to those built in Devon and Cornwall, as no fort of this type had been examined in Wales. The excavations revealed that the bank was built with rubble with a dry-stone wall on the outside to give support to the outer face and help retain its vertical aspect. The entrance to the main enclosure is on the north-east side, and now appears as a gap where this outer scarp meets the main bank. Excavations show that the entrance was cobbled and its sides stone-lined, as large blocks found in the ditch probably formed a revetment near the lip of the ditch. The entrance was closed by gates supported on four large posts, of which the excavated holes can still be seen in the corners.[84]

Inside the fort the remains of two round huts were found and further excavation might reveal more. The hut adjacent to the rampart on the north-west side had been occupied by a building which measured about 7m in diameter with low walls built of earth and rock. The roof had been supported by 6 or 7 posts. A few pieces of Middle Iron Age pottery, which has been dated to 100-50 BC, lay on the floor. The large hut near the middle of the enclosure produced no finds, but revealed a number of post holes. These could have represented two phases of construction, the earlier being a round house, 10m in diameter. The four main rafters met in the middle, and were supported by four massive posts set at four points on the circumference of the hut, their outer ends lying on the ground rock platform outside the hut's walls. Later, the platform seems to have carried a further three pairs of posts, which perhaps represent drying-racks. A little to the south of the northernmost hut, a further hut platform was found but left un-excavated.

Just to the east of the summit of Hardings Down is a semicircular rampart that appears to be an unfinished hillfort (SS 437 906). A short stretch of isolated bank on the west side indicates its intended length and shows it was near to completion. There is no trace of a ditch where the banks are absent, but a short isolated stretch of rampart indicates approximately the position of the west end. The entrance through the outer rampart is seen as a simple gap with a barely visible hollow track leading from it to the main rampart. The bank on the south side is slightly thickened and there is a levelled annexe behind it which may have been intended to house animals.

To the north of the summit is a small circular fortified enclosure. It is surrounded by a bank and a ditch with a counterscarp bank (SS 437 908). This smaller fort would appear to have been a defended homestead for one or perhaps a few families. Its entrance is on the north-west side and is approached by a hollow between the stony banks. Inside the enclosure there is one circular hut platform on the east side up against the bank, but which has not been excavated.

The whole of the Hardings Down site is a mystery with many unanswered questions. Why were three forts built in close proximity? Were they built at the same time? The location of the two smaller forts on the side of the hill suggests that the summit fort was already there, but if that were the case, why start to build another two instead of finishing off the first? The lack of huts within the two completed forts suggests that these substantial earthworks sheltered only one or two families, rather than a larger community, but why?

South-east of Hardings Down on Druids Moor (SS 441 901) there is an enclosure similar to the small circular fort. Here, the oval-shaped enclosure stands on water-logged ground surrounded by a bank and external ditch. There is a 3m wide entrance on the east-south-east side. Little is known as again the site has never been excavated.

Legend informs us that the occupants of Hardings Down met those of nearby Bulwark for a battle on open ground, now known as Tankeylake Moor. It is claimed that it was a particularly brutal battle and many lives were lost, and Tonkin, the leader of the Bulwark fort, was killed. The slaughter was apparently so great and with much blood shed that the blood flowed over the great warrior's boots, hence the name Tankey (or Tonkin) Lake.

The Bulwark

Hillfort
Location: Just south of Llanmadoc (SS 443 928)
Access: By public footpath

Take the signposted footpath up the hill from the edge of the village of Llanmadoc. The fort is located on the end of the ridge.

For some unknown reason the people who occupied the fortified settlement called The Bulwark, like their neighbours on Hardings Down, built their fort away from the summit on ground sloping down hill. Certainly it was not an ideal defensive position, so there may be other reasons for this choice of site. The grass-covered rubble banks and rock-cut ditches form a very complex pattern of multiple defences on the ground. It can only be fully appreciated by looking at a plan or an aerial photograph, then it becomes obvious that the fort has been developed over several periods.

This site has an inner oval-shaped enclosure of some 0.9 hectares surrounded by a bank and ditch, with an entrance gap on the east side. A trackway bordered by additional ramparts leads up the hill to the gate. Almost surrounding this is a second line of defensive banks and ditches, which was never completed on the steeply sloping north-east side. Yet another rampart and ditch has been cut across the collar of the ridge on the more level western approach. The reason for this can only be assumed, and it may have been that the hillfort builders had intended this outer bank to run around the entire southern edge of the hill, and finally link up with the defence work on the east side. No large scale excavations have been carried out at the site, although a small excavation, carried out by A.G. Davies in 1957 suggested that there were two periods of construction on the rampart on the north-west corner of the fort.[85] Earlier, in the 1870s, J.D. Davies dug up some animal bones, charcoal and stone implements. The main feature visible today inside the fort is a small bank and ditch cutting off a sub-rectangular enclosure in the south-eastern corner with an entrance to the north-east. This has been interpreted as an animal annexe. To the west the ground is uneven which suggests that huts existed here but nothing has been uncovered to validate this.

Cil Ifor Top

Hillfort
Location: Llanrhidian (SS 505 923)
Access: On private ground, but can be viewed
from nearby roads

There are several good vantage points along the B4295 and from a minor road onto Welsh Moor.

Cil Ifor Top is the largest hillfort on the Gower Peninsula, occupying almost 3 hectares, and follows the natural contours of the hill. Sadly, centuries of cultivation and erosion by the weather have largely destroyed the defences. It was probably an important encampment during its heyday because the complex entrances were all fitted with timber barricades and pointed stakes.

Excavations by William Morgan in 1910 revealed that beneath the earthworks were rock-cut ditches up to 2.5m thick. No artefacts to aid dating were found, although he described red pottery which could have been Roman Samian ware, which was mass produced in Gaul.[86]

In the middle of the western end of the enclosure are indications of several hut platforms. The interior is now entirely pasture although, in an undisturbed part, three hut platforms survive and there are indications of two or possibly three more. The only entrance is on the south-west side where the ground slopes steeply upwards to what is now a simple gap.

Nothing is known of its history. However, Cil is Welsh for 'retreat' and perhaps the site was used over the centuries as a place to seek safety. Perhaps parts of the ditches were roofed with branches overlaid with turf or hide to provide temporary shelters.

Burry Holms

Promontory fort
Location: On Burry Holms, northern end of Rhossili Bay
(SS 399 926)
Access: Across the beach at low tide

At Llangenydd take the minor road north-west to the Burrows. You can park at the end of the road and walk 1.5km to the headland.

Burry Holms fort possesses a marvellous natural defence, for at high tide the headland becomes an island.

The highest part of the headland was fortified by a high bank, ditch and outer counterscarp bank. The bank runs in a north-south direction straight across the headland, and the ditch makes use of a natural fault in the landscape. The entrance is a simple gap with a causeway across the ditch in the middle of the bank.

The island site is more famous for its later connections with Christianity and St. Cenydd, Gower's own saint. In 1965, during excavations on the ecclesiastical site, a section was cut across the Iron Age 'rampart' which was found to be of solid rock just left of the entrance.[87] The ditch was a blunt V-shape, about 0.7m deeper than the present bottom. Below the ecclesiastical remains there was an extensive layer of discoloured soil of calcined stone, possibly indicating the dwelling place of the Iron Age occupants of the fort, but no finds of pottery were discovered to substantiate this.

High Pennard & Bishopston

Two promontory forts
Location: High Pennard: 2km south-west of Bishopston (SS 567
866); Bishopston: 1km along Bishopston Valley (SS 569 878)
Access: By public footpath, though these can be difficult and
overgrown in the latter case

Access to High Pennard can be had from the car park at the
southern end of Southgate, along the coastal path, whilst
Bishopston hillfort can be reached from the coast path at Pwll-du
Bay, along a path up Bishopston Valley. About 1km along the valley
there is a sharp right turn, sitting on the ridge above the bend is the
very overgrown Bishopston promontory fort.

The cliff on the south and west side of High Pennard fort made
artificial protection on these sides unnecessary. The summit of the
promontory is divided into two by natural cliffs so that the area is
enclosed by the man-made defences on two separate levels.
Excavations by Audrey Williams in 1939 revealed that a single
bank and ditch cut off the lower part and it was here that the excavators found the remains of two hut sites. They also discovered that
the upper section was more effectively defended by a line of double
banks and ditches on the landward side. The excavation concen-
trated on the inner rampart which revealed a timber gateway along
with a 'guard hut' just inside the entrance. The most interesting
feature was a rock-cut gully or drain leading from within the
rampart to a pit. For what it was used is unknown, but it could have
been designed to collect water for drinking purposes. A chance find
of a clay spindle-whorl indicates that weaving took place at this
site. This and other finds are now at Swansea Museum.
Interestingly this fort was known in 1729 for other reasons, because
the cartographer Emmanuel Bowen thought it significant enough to
include it in his map of South Wales, although he drew it is as a star-
shaped artillery fort!

Bishopston was excavated at the same time as High Pennard. On
the north-west of the entrance an oval hollow 4m by 3m, filled with
dark soil, was discovered. This was apparently the site of a midden

rather than a hut. Other finds included two slingstones, bones of red deer, ox, pig and sheep or goat, as well as shells of dog-whelk, limpet, mussel, periwinkle and snails which indicate a mixed economy of farming, gathering, fishing and hunting. Other chance finds include a bronze penannual brooch of Roman date, and an iron finger ring. A sherd of middle to late Iron Age pottery, and a fragment of a plain Samian ware of the late first to second centuries AD suggest that the fort was also probably occupied by a Celtic family during Roman times. A hut was located just behind the inner rampart, but despite several digs within the enclosure, no other dwellings or finds have come to light.

Thurba

Promontory fort
Location: Near Rhossili (SS 422 820)
Access: By public footpath along the coast

The coastal footpath can be reached from a variety of places, including Rhossili, Middleton, Pitton, Pitton Green, Port-Eynon and Overton.

The stretch of rocky coast between Worm's Head and Port Eynon Point is rich in small defended forts on tops of the cliffs. The most important ones are Thurba, The Knave, Paviland and Horse Cliff. All have similarities, although this particular rocky headland would appear to be an inhospitable place to live. Although the rock is naturally strong, the headland is far from level being broken in places by clifftop and steep craggy slopes. The builders of this fort took full advantage of the landscape so that they could channel any unwanted invaders along a narrow shelf below the ramparts. Any attackers who succeeded in avoiding missiles hurled from the fort would have then faced an uphill climb to the entrance.

Thurba is defended on the landward side by a series of ditches and banks, although the outermost rampart is now reduced to just a steep slope on the north-west side, and a rubble bank with a faint outer ditch on the east. The main defence lies behind this and consists of a substantial bank and ditch. Within this runs a wall along the edge of the summit which may represent a small inner enclosure which was possibly an earlier fort, with the more extensive outer ramparts added later. A further stretch of similar walling about 3m thick is blocking a possible entrance from the south. Any remains to be found on the south side are now obscured by quarrying and an old limekiln. Within the enclosure are shallow hollows with level floors ranging from 3m to 6m across. The two hollows adjacent to the stone wall are almost certainly hut sites, and the other three are probably so. No hut sites have been found on the north or south slopes and no major excavation has taken place on the site.

The Knave

Promontory fort
Location: About 2km south-east of Rhossili (SS 432 864)
Access: Along the coastal path

This fort has sometimes been given the name of Deborah's Hole Camp, and sits to the east of Thurba fort. Its defences are semicircular in shape and cut off an area of about half a hectare on the clifftop, just west of the broken cliffs known as the Knave. On the landward side there is a double arc consisting of a bank and outer ditch. The inner bank is highest and reaches a height of nearly 3m at its eastern end. The entrances in both semicircles are at the west end and the area enclosed measures about 0.1 hectare. The ramparts, which today are much overgrown, are considerably reduced in size because of erosion and stone robbing but, in its day, was a formidable defence with thick rubble banks lined with a dry stone wall.

The site was excavated in 1938 by Mrs. Audrey Williams and the remains of two wattle and daub round huts were found. One was positioned in the angle of the bank and was possibly used as a guardroom. The second was located near the cliff edge and had been burnt down. Amongst the finds were fragments of Iron Age pottery and pot-boilers—stones which were heated and then plunged into water to heat it. There was also a selection of shells, bones of sheep or goats and oxen, as well as slingstones. The ramparts were also investigated and the inner bank was found to have been lined on the inside with squarish blocks and on the outside with rough boulders. The outer bank was more crudely lined with stone, and its external V-shaped ditch was rock-cut. Excavation of the outermost entrance revealed a line of three post-holes which suggests that there were two wooden gates, hung on side posts and closed against a central upright pole.

The Knave, Horse Cliff and Paviland forts are extremely close to each other, notably the latter two, which is quite fascinating. They are quite small, giving space for only a dwelling, a couple of storage huts and an enclosed 'yard'; not really sufficient to be considered highly defensible, but certainly enough to ensure that stock remained inside and could not easily be purloined. The nearest equivalent are the 17th-19th century estate farms, where each was responsible for a small area under the control of the local big landowner. If this was the case here in the Iron Age, it would indicate more an agricultural race than a warrior one.

Horse Cliff Fort

Promontory fort
Location: about 2.5km south-east of Rhossili (SS 434 860)
Access: Along the coastal path from Rhossili, Pitton Green
or Port Eynon

This defended homestead, to the west of the Paviland fort, is extremely well chosen, although rather bleak and exposed. The defences occupy the east end of the narrow headland and would have entailed minimum effort on the part of the builders. It consists of a single grass-grown bank of limestone rubble, curving to the east and fronted on the landward side by a simple ditch. The photograph shows the bank and ditch, looking roughly west-north-west towards Worm's Head in the distance. Although the site is badly eroded there is enough of the curve surviving to trace it to the cliff edge. On the south side it ends abruptly, about 5m short of the edge and a gap in the defences clearly indicate that this was the entrance. At this point the bank turns inwards and it has been suggested that a guard-chamber would have been present within the turn.[88]

Paviland

Promontory fort
Location: About 2.5km south-east of Rhossili (SS 437 860)
Access: Along the coastal path from Rhossili, Pitton Green
or Port Eynon

This is yet another of the series of small cliff top forts that dominate the landscape between Worm's Head and Port Eynon. It sits on the top of a long, narrow headland, with deep valleys on either side and a sheer cliff on the seaward side, in which Goat's Cave is located. The photograph shows the level platform of the 'fort' in the middle distance with banks to each side.

Here there are four lines of defence and a selection of slingstones recovered indicate its importance as a defensive fort. On the seaward side a small area has been enclosed by an impressive bank of rubble limestone outside of which there is a natural depression. Within the enclosed area are rough platforms, possible hut sites, which are the only signs of habitation. Further away from the seaward side are three further lines of defence, the first being apparently an unfinished rock-cut ditch. The second is a shallow ditch with a low bank inside it and entrance towards the east end. The third and outermost line is a larger bank, again of limestone rubble, with an external ditch. The entrance may have been at the northern end.

Glossary of Terms

Assemblage: A Group of artefacts related to each other and based on recovery in a common archaeological context *i.e.* from the same site.

Barrow: Round or long mound of earth or turf constructed over a burial chamber and particular to the Bronze Age. There are many different shapes surrounded by a ditch and were usually used as a final resting place for more than one person.

Beaker People: People who first entered Britain around 2600 BC, their name coming from the distinctive and elegant pots that were often buried with the dead under round barrows. They may have also been the first metal users in Britain.

Bronze: Alloy of copper mixed with tin or lead.

Burial Chamber: The burial or funerary chamber, constructed of stone or wood of large dimensions—which distinguish it from a cist. The chamber usually contained the resting place of more than one person.

Cairn: A round or elongated mound of stone, often covering a chamber or burial of Bronze Age date.

Capstone: The horizontal stone on top of the chamber, passage or Dolmen.

Chambered Cairn: A chambered tomb which is covered with stones.

Cist: A small box-like square or rectangular burial place.

Chert: A very fine grained rock formed in ancient sea sediments. It usually has a semi-glassy finish and is normally white, pinkish, brown, grey or blue-grey in colour. In was shaped into arrowheads by chipping, and has often been mistaken for flint. True flint is found in chalk deposits and is a distinctive blackish translucent colour.

Counterscarp bank: A additional bank crowning the outer slope of the ditch of a hillfort.

Dolmen: Simple megalithic burial chamber with three or more uprights and one or more capstones.

End Scraper: A stone tool formed by chipping the end of a flake of stone which can then be used to scrape animal hides and wood.

Flint: A hard glassy rock which flakes off easily and can be worked to produce a sharp cutting edge. Used in prehistoric times for the manufacture of tools and weapons such as scrapers and arrowheads.

Forecourt: The space in the front of certain British, Iberian and Italian monuments.

Grave Goods: The funeral offerings placed inside or near a tomb. These are often the only means of establishing the date of construction of a monument.

Henge: A circular enclosure formed by an earthen bank and ditch (usually internal) which are almost unique to the British Late Neolithic period.

Incised: A decoration found on pottery consisting of lines drawn into wet clay. When fired, the arrangement of lines leaves a permanent design on the vessel surface.

Inhumation: The burial of the dead body. The position of the corpse may be extended, flexed or crouched, and prone, supine or on its side.

Kerb: A ring or retaining stones against a mound or a cairn base.

Lynchet: A ridge or ledge formed by soil creep due to ploughing on a slope over a number of years.

Megalith: From the Greek word 'great stone' and is sometimes wrongly used to describe a megalithic monument.

Mesolithic: The middle Stone Age period—the period between the Palaeolithic and the Neolithic, from 7000 BC to 4500 BC.

Midden: A layer of soil which contains the by-products of human activity as the result of an accumulation of these materials on their living surface. This is seen as a layer of soil, stained dark, by the decomposition of organic refuse which also contained food bones, fragments of stone tools, charcoal, pieces of pottery and other discarded items.

Neolithic: The period when nomadic life moved to a more settled farming way of life, around 4500 BC to 2200 BC.

Orthostat: Large stone of slab which has been set vertically in a structure.

Palaeolithic: Old Stone Age, which begins around 500,000 years ago and ends with the Mesolithic Age, around 7000 BC.

Quartzite: A stone which was formed in water deposited sediments and consists of sand grains which have been cemented together. It can be chipped, but is very difficult to work.

Sherds: The individual pieces of broken pottery.

Tumulus: Latin for a mound or a barrow and generally covers one burial.

Appendix 1

Guide to the main sites in Gower and West Glamorgan

Name	Grid ref

Caves - Palaeolithic and later

Goat's Hole, Paviland	437 859
Tooth Cave	531 909
Kittle Hill	577 894
Bacon Hole	561 868
Minchin Hole	555 868
Leather's Hole	530 877
Long Hole	452 851
Deborah's Hole	433 863
Mewslade caves	423 873
Bosco's Den	426 937
Worm's Head Cave	383 877
Culver Hole	405 929
Spritsail Tor	426 937
North Hill Tor	453 938
Crow Hole	558 869
Caswell Bay Cave	589 879
Cwtch Cave	432 863
Port Eynon Point	468 844
Mumbles Hill Cave	625 875
Ravencliff Cave	547 873
Rother's Tor Cave	609 874
Cat Hole Cave	538 901
Burry Holms	399 925
Lesser Garth Cave	125 821

Neolithic Tombs

Parc le Breos	537 898
Penmaen Burrows	532 881
Nicholaston Long Cairn	507 888
Arthur's Stone	491 905

Sweyne's Howes South	420 898
Sweyne's Howes North	421 899
Carn Llechart	697 063

Bronze Age Cairns and Circles

Great Cairn Cefn Bryn	490 904
Group of Cairns Cefn Bryn	409 490, 492 902, 993 903
Group of Cairns Rhossili Down	421 897, 420 890, 418 900
Burry Holms	398 926
Group of Cairns Llanmadoc Hill	430 927, 440 927
Carn Llechart	698 062
Carn Goch	605 980
Penlle'rbebyll	635 048
Merthyr Mawr Warren	850 770, 855 768, 859 770
Pen-y-Crug	510 913
Bishopston Burch	571 909
Graig Fawr Ring Cairn	628 066

Bronze Age Standing Stones

Burry Group of Stones	464 900, 463 900, 469 891
Samson's Jack	475 916
Carreg Bica	724 994

Iron Age Hillforts and Settlements

High Pennard	567 866
Bishopston Valley	569 878
Horse Cliff	434 860
The Knave	432 864
Thurba Head	422 820
Paviland	473 860
Burry Holms	933 926
The Bulwarks	443 928
Cil ifor Top	505 923
Druid's Moor	441 901
Hardings Down	434 908, 437 906, 437 908
Llyn Fawr	917 035
Buarth Maen	012 053
Carreg Lwyd	922 018

Bibliography

Cunliffe, Barry *Celtic World*, Constable

Daniel, G.E. *The Prehistoric Chamber Tombs of England & Wales*, Cambridge, 1950

Davies. J.D. *The History of West Wales*, 4 Vols., 1877, 1879, 1885, 1894

Fox, C. *Life and Death in the Bronze Age*, London, 1959

Green, Miranda J. (ed.) *The Celtic World*, Routledge

Green, Miranda J. *Dictionary of Celtic Myth and Legend*, Thames and Hudson

Hamon, Isaac *Description of Gower 1697* (reprinted in Transactions of the Cymmrodorion, 1965)

James, David (ed.) *Celtic Connections*, Blandford

Jones, J. Graham *The Pocket Guide History of Wales*, University of Wales Press

Koch, John (ed.) *The Celtic Heroic Age—Literary Sources*, Celtic Studies Publications, Massachusetts

Lambert, David *Cambridge Guide to Prehistoric Man*

Mackenzie, Donald *Ancient Man in Britain*, Blackie and Sons

Morris, B. *Caves of Gower*, Gower Society, 1971

Pearson, Michael Parker *Bronze Age Britain*, English Heritage

Powell, T.G.E. *et al Megalithic Enquiries in the West of Britain*, Liverpool, 1969

RCAHM *Glamorgan* Vol.1 parts 1 and 2

Stewart, R.J. *Celtic Gods, Celtic Goddesses*, Blandford

Time Life Books *Neanderthals*, Time Life

Wheeler, R.E.M. *Prehistoric and Roman Wales*, Clarendon Press

Whittle, Elizabeth *A Guide to Ancient and Historic Wales - Glamorgan and Gwent*, CADW

Endnotes

Abbreviations
Arch. Camb. for *Archaeologia Cambrensis*
BBCS for *Bulletin of the Board of Celtic Studies*
Gower for *The Journal of the Gower Society*

1. A.D. Lacille, *Ant. Journal* XXXIV 1954
2. *Coygan Camp - a prehistoric, Romano-British and Dark Age settlement in Carmarthenshire*, G.J. Wainwright, 1967
3. *A Guide to Ancient and Historic Wales - Glamorgan and Gwent*, Elizabeth Whittle, CADW
4. Paviland Cave: an Aurignacian Station, Wales, Huxley Memorial Lecture for 1913
5. Reported by Starling Benson in Ann. Rep. Swansea Lit. and Sci Soc., 1852, p.9
6. *Excavations on Defence Sites 1939-45: Neolithic and Bronze Age*, W.F. Grimes, HMSO, 1960
7. *Prehistoric Gower*, Rutter
8. *Arch. Camb.* CXVII 1968 pp. 28-31
9. *Trans. Cardiff Nat. Soc.* LXXXIX 1959-1960 pp. 9-30
10. Williams 'Clegyr Boia, St David's, Pembrokeshire: Excavations in 1943' in *Arch. Camb.* No.102, pp20-47
11. *British Archaeology* no.12, March 1996
12. *BBCS* XVI, iii Nov 1955, p. 228
13. J.W. Lukis, *Arch. Camb.*, 1875, pp. 173-4
14. *Gower* XXXII pp. 47-52
15. *Gower* XXXIII
16. *Journal of the Royal Anthropological Institute* Vol XLIII, 1913
17. Palaeanthological memoirs and notes pp. 538-40
18. Ex. Inf. J.B. Campbell
19. Plan and section by H. Hussey in *Arch. Camb.*, 1887 pp. 200-1
20. *Proc. Prehist. Soc.*, XXV 1959 pp. 265-8
21. Ex. Inf. J.B. Campbell
22. *Proc. Geol. Ass.* XLIII 1932, p. 297
23. *BBCS* XXII ii Nov 1967, pp. 277-90
24. *Arch. Camb.*, 1871, pp. 168-72
25. *Needles of Stone*, T. Graves, London, 1978
26. *Arch. Camb.* 1870, pp. 25-39, 39
27. Iolo Morganwg Welsh Manuscripts Society, Llandovery, 1848, pp. 83, 473

28. *Arch. Camb.,* 1870
29. Sir Norman Lockyer, Address to the Royal Institute South Wales, 1908
30. *Arch. Camb.,* 1870, facing pp. 120
31. *Proc. Prehist. Soc.,* VI, 1940, pp. 178-81
32. *Arch. Camb.,* 1894, pp. 1-7, and again, in greater detail, in *Tran. Swansea Sci. Soc.,* 1892- 3, p. 54
33. *The Bronze Age and the Celtic World,* H.J.E Peake, p. 36
34. *Arch. Camb.,* 1871, p. 327
35. *Arch. Camb.,* 1919, p. 338
36. *Arch. Camb.,* XCIV, 1939, p. 22
37. *Journ. Roy. Soc. Ant. Ireland,* LXXXIV, 1954, pp. 105-55
38. *Trans. Cardiff Nat. Soc.,* XLVII, 1914, op. p. 11
39. *Arch. Camb.,* 1919, pp. 336-47, VCIV, 1939
40. *Trans. Cardiff Nat. Soc.,* LXXXVII, 1933, p. 38
41. *BBCS,* XV iv, May 1954, p. 394
42. *Arch. Camb.,* XCVIII, 1944, pp. 53-7)
43. *Arch. Camb.,* XCVIII, 1944, pp. 57-63
44. Mumbles Press Oct. 1929
45. Morganwg, XIII, 1969, pp. 108-100
46. M.S. Hussey *Trans. Cardiff Nat. Soc.* XCIII 1964-6 pp. 18-39
47. *BBCS,* VII, Nov. 1931, pp. 90-2; VIII, May 1932, pp. 196-7; and VII iv, May 1935, pp. 417-18
48. *Bronze Age Britain,* Michael Parker Pearson, 1994
49. *BBCS,* VIII, iii, Nov 1936, p. 274; and *Arch. Camb.,* XCVII, 1942, p. 91
50. *Arch. Camb.,* XCII, 1937; and BBCS, IX iii, Nov. 1938, p. 285
51. *Arch. Camb.,* XCVII, 1942, pp. 77-92
52. *Arch. Camb.,* CIII, 1954, pp. 66-84
53. *Stone Circles of the British Isles,* A. Burl
54. *BBCS,* XXI iii, Nov. 1965, pp. 250-4
55. *Stone Implements* (2nd Edition), S.S. Evans, p. 187
56. *Arch. Camb.,* 1866, p. 100
57. *Arch. Camb.,* 1856, p. 136
58. *Arch. Camb.,* XCIV, 1939, p. 22
59. *Gower* II; Davies, p. 72
60. *Arch. Camb.,* XCIV, 1939, p. 22; and BBCS, XVII iii, Nov. 1957
61. *Gower* XXXII, XXXIII
62. *Arch. Camb.,* 1879, p. 27
63. *BBCS,* XIII, May, 1949 pp. 110-111
64. *Gower* XIII, 1960, p. 65

65. *Prehistoric Gower*, Rutter, p. 47
66. Glamorgan & Gwent Archaeology Trust. Sites and Monuments Records
67. Grimes in *Proceedings of the Neath Antiquarian Society*, 1938
68. *Folklore of the Afan District*, Martin Phillips, Bridgend, 1938
69. *East Gower,* Rutter and Allen, pp. 31-2
70. *Prehistoric Gower*, Rutter, p. 56
71. 'Some Late Bronze Age Hoards' in *Archaeologia Atlantic* 1 (2) by H.N. Savory, 1975; *A Guide Catalogue to the Iron Age Collections, Cardiff*, National Museum of Wales, 1976
72. 'Cross Channel Relations in the Later Bronze Age' in *British Archaeological Reports International Series* no.91, by B. O'Conner, Oxford, 1980
73. 'The Severn Sisters Hoard, a centenary study' in *Welsh Antiquity* by Davies and Spratling, 1976, p.121-48
74. R.A. Smith in *Proc. Soc. Ant.* 2nd series XX p.189
75. *Arch. Camb.*, XI, iii, appendix
76. H.N. Savory, 'A Review of Cunlesse 1988: Greeks, Romans and Barbarians: Spheres of Interaction' in *Arch. Camb.*, 139, 1990, pp.82-3
77. The pot: H.N. Savory 1976 - Early Iron Age Collection Cardiff; the mould: *Arch. Camb.*, 123, 1974, pp. 170-4
78. *Arch. Camb.*, 1927, pp. 44-66
79. *BBCS*, Nov. 11 1921
80. *History* XXIII, Livy
81. *Celtic Connections*, David James and Simant Bostock, 1996
82. Koch, John (ed.) *The Celtic Heroic Age—Literary Sources*, Celtic Studies Publications, Massachusetts, 82, 2.17, 8-12
83. *The Story of British Coinage,* Peter Seaby
84. Excavations at Hardings Down West Fort, Hogg, in *Arch. Camb.*, 122, 1973, pp. 55-68
85. *BBCS*, XXI i, Nov. 1964, p. 100
86. *Trans. Swansea Sci. Soc.*, 1910-11, p. 133
87. D.B. Hague, *Gower* XV11, 1966
88. *BBCS*, VIII iv, May 1937, p. 365; and *Prehistoric Gower*, Rutter, p. 65